YOU ARE WHAT YOU WEAR

The Science of the
Motion Picture and Television
Wardrobe Department

WILLIAM THOURLBY

FORBES/WITTENBURG & BROWN

Forbes/Wittenburg & Brown
250 West 57th Street, Suite 1527
New York, New York 10107

ISBN: 0-945429-00-2
Library of Congress Catalog Card Number: 88-91194

This is the new and expanded edition of the original hard cover edition published by Andrews and McMeel, Inc.

*"You Are What You Wear" is available at quantity discounts when used to promote products, services or corporate training departments. For information please write to Premium Marketing Division, Forbes/Wittenburg and Brown, **250 West 57th Street, Suite 1527, New York, New York 10107***

Printed in the United States of America
20 19 18 17 16 15 14 13 12

To my daughters
  Jamie Patricia
  Abby Carole
  Nana Leigh
  Liza Grace
For they give my life its worth and direction

Contents

Acknowledgments

Many people (friends, customers, sometimes strangers, chance acquaintances) have contributed both consciously and unconsciously to the content of this book. All these people I thank; a few I want to take this opportunity to give special acknowledgement: Donna Dale Stephens for never complaining about the massive typing and retyping; my friend Joseph McElligott whose many skills were always there when I needed them; Rebecca James for her dedication to her work and the contribution of her drawings. Thanks to my friend Nelson Buhler who made it all possible. And, of course, thanks to Jim Andrews, John McMeel and Tom Drape at Andrews and McMeel for their faith.

PREFACE

When "You Are What You Wear" was first published, the fashion industry was quick to criticize what they saw as a conformist, in-stylish philosophy of dress. My thesis went against the grain of trendy, extreme clothing, and in its simplicity, challenged the foundation of the fashion pacesetters — which is change. I spoke out against sacred cows: novelty, adventurous colors, radical alterations in silhouette. Well, change is the life blood (and profit) of the fashion conglomerates, and my intractable conservatism was a threat to their pocket books.

What a difference a decade makes! Now the industry speaks my language: investment clothing, classic clothing, business clothing, down time, outer wear clothing, and ranging above all like an anthem, "You Are What You Wear." Although it was not perceived at once, time has shown that everyone in the industry has benefited from the book's ideas. Maybe a young executive following my precepts will purchase fewer suits, but those suits will be of top quality, as the accessories will also be. There is not an anti-fashion bias in the book, only a pro-conservative insistence. And from the comments I have received from letters and during seminars, I am convinced that the book has served as a functional guide to many thousands of men who have accepted the dictum that their appearance strongly influences how high they can aspire on the corporate ladder.

"You Are What You Wear" also probes deeper than fabric and design. I have also tried to present a practical working philosophy which encompasses major points of how to advance and develop as a person as well as a corporate leader. One of my treasured moments resulting from the publication of the book came to me while I was running my seminar at the great Brigham Young University in Provo, Utah. The seminar had been a great success; the questions and answer period just kept going on and on. It was supposed to be over by 9:30; by 10:30 there were still people and questions. Finally three people came walking up. A young man held out his hand and said, "Mr. Thourlby, I drove 150 miles to be here tonight, and my friend and his wife wanted to meet you too." The four of us went to a late coffee joint and talked. He poured out his story. Modest background, the pain and strain of trying to get it all together and get it going. As he unfolded his story I witnessed a beautiful human being, who had been able to accept pain as part of humanity and had not become its victim. Instead, making them growing pains. And he had turned them into learning experiences. He said, "You Are What You Wear" was the Catalyst for his life. "It pulled it all together and packaged the product for me."

We stood there saying goodbye. I was proud of the book, proud of my new friend, and in the process, became a better person for the experience.

Introduction

Today it seems that everyone is searching for a way to change their lives. The bookstores are crowded with volumes dealing with positive mental attitudes, motivation, and even self-deception to change one's life. Psychologists amass large fortunes by instructing people to like themselves better, tell themselves they are O.K., and even how to think and grow rich. Unfortunately, there are a few, hard facts that must be faced. First, you can't change your background and development. You can't go back and get a new set of parents. You can't change the way you were brought up. You can't exchange your height or mental equipment for a new model. Few of you can drop everything and return to school for a new education and new career. Bleak as it seems, there is one simple thing that you can alter and thereby dramatically change your life. You can change your appearance, by packaging yourself to achieve specific goals, and become happier, successful, and even richer. The reason is actually a simple and logical one. to the people you meet and deal with in everyday life, "You Are What You Wear."

As you read this book and begin to understand the above concept, you'll see that the clothing you wear, which covers up 90 percent of your body, dominates your business and social relationships. You'll start to consciously plan your appearance to alter the way people interact with you. As you realize that people you meet automatically accept the role you package yourself for, you'll completely turn around in your thinking. You'll understand that the way you dress can determine how far you go in life. In fact, I guarantee you this, whether you like it or not, after reading this book your life will never be the same.

With the tremendous body of literature available concerning how appearance affects the social and business aspects of life, I had to resist the temptation to let this treatise turn into a textbook or scholarly tome. Sociologists, social-psychologists, anthropologists, and many other types of scientists have long studied the relationship between dress and social interaction. I, as an author, have attempted to interpret and explain their findings in light of my own specialized and unique background. Although I occasionally cite specific studies to illuminate particularly important points, I have endeavored to write an easily understood, practical, guide for the man who wants to use his appearance as another tool in his climb to success. If I succeed in helping you understand that "You Are What You Wear," to those whom you meet, and make you begin to analyze what your clothes say about you, then I have accomplished my main task. I'm not suggesting that you must follow the recommendations contained herein, simply that you understand what your clothes say about you. It's then up to you to package yourself depending upon the priorities you set for yourself, to say what you want about yourself.

The combined experiences of twenty-five years as a professional actor, model, clothier and creator of Emory University's course *You Are What You Wear* have helped me to develop a clear understanding of the value of an appropriate image and first impression in addition to the mechanics of acquiring, presenting, and managing it.

On stage and in films the social, economical, educational, and even the moral status of stage and film characters is conveyed to audiences through their dress, even before the first word of dialogue is spoken. I first became interested in the tremendous influence that clothing and appearance have on our lives when I noticed actors arriving for work at the movie studios looking for all the world like people from the wrong side of the tracks, yet being miraculously packaged by the wardrobe department to portray just the opposite convincingly. The effect of wardrobe was awesome, yet most actors failed to realize its significance.

While working with a wardrobe man, I was amazed when he matter-of-factly mentioned that the really aware actors began to package themselves for their private lives based on the positive reinforcements they received in their roles. It wasn't until much later that I learned through studying psychology that you could actually become what you wear. As you shall see, the way you package yourself with your clothing and appearance can dramatically change your life.

It was during the same time that *Esquire* magazine began the production of a film entitled *The Image of a Man*. It was the first motivational research film on men's clothing. I was intensely interested in it because I had already become aware of image impact and wanted to know more. *Esquire* had been looking for an actor to do the film and because of my keen interest in the subject the director, Carl Ficke, hired me. I was fascinated. I began searching for more data on the impact of image. What I discovered was an entire technology which was being applied in the studio and laboratories and never getting out in the street where people needed it most.

I looked further. I spent every available minute talking to wardrobe people, to tailors, clothiers, and others, trying to get a fresh viewpoint on this. Packaging people, the motivational research experts, and others shared their secrets with me. Over the next ten years I devoted more and more time to the science of wardrobe, and less and less time to acting.

Soon the transition was complete. I decided to devote my energies to helping others learn to use and apply this technology. I left Hollywood and returned to New York to open my first men's shop on Forty Sixth Street, just off Fifth Avenue. A year later I sold the shop in New York, moved to Atlanta, and began to apply this technology in earnest.

Then I began a series of speaking engagements and consultations for businesses and businessmen to teach them what their clothes were saying about them, professionally and socially. A Department Head attended one of my seminars and invited me to design a course for Emory University. I called the course *You Are What You Wear* . . . because you are! The course was an eye-opener. I'd expected it to be attended by students. Instead, it was filled with doctors, lawyers, salesmen, and accountants—successful men wondering why they had hit their career plateaus instead of moving up. By the end of the year I proved to them that the reactions elicited by the clothing we wear opens and closes doors at the top—professionally, socially, and economically.

My students began to clamor for a handbook, a manual, or anything they could use as a reference for the materials we covered in the course lectures. I began receiving similar requests from executives and corporations who had tried unsuccessfully to convince their employees of the same phenomenon. You *can* change your life by changing your appearance. For anyone looking for a future beyond the armed services where everyone wears a uniform, I recommend this book.

The apparel oft proclaims the man.
— Shakespeare

1

YOU ARE WHAT YOU WEAR

When you step into a room, even though no one in that room knows you or has seen you before, they will make ten decisions about you based solely on your appearance. They may make more, but you can be assured that they will make these:

1. Your economic level
2. Your educational level
3. Your trustworthiness
4. Your social position
5. Your level of sophistication
6. Your economic heritage
7. Your social heritage
8. Your educational heritage
9. Your success
10. Your moral character

To be successful in almost any endeavor, you must be sure that these decisions about you are favorable, because in that first impression you make—you are what you wear. If you realize that your inner image is reflected in what covers up

90 percent of you—your wardrobe—you'll be able to take advantage of the situation.

Let's take a look at just what people really assume about you from your appearance.

Realize first that you are given a shape, a height, a color and appearance by a power greater than your own. Your challenge is to take what has been given you and make it interesting and desirable. You, like most young men, went through twelve years of high school, struggling and frustrated. Perhaps you were fortunate enough to cram, hustle, and hope through four or five years of college. Then, you went out into the world in your chosen profession or job. You probably joined a large company and were advised by the "Old Guard" to join the Toastmaster's Club, take the Dale Carnegie Course and, once the shuttling had stopped, to take several in-company courses. Perhaps your career path was slightly different but the point to be made is that very few of you ever had the facts of life explained to you with regard to the impression you made on your associates, customers, or superiors.

Consider for a moment that once you get that piece of paper which says you have an education, no one is going to write your college to see if you cheated, or had your girl friend write your term papers. Think about it! When you chose your family doctor, did you find out what medical school he attended? Would it have mattered if you did? Did you write for a transcript of his grades in surgical skills or diagnosing? When you selected your lawyer, did you write his law school to find out his grades in moot court or how well he wrote for the *Journal*? Actually, no one does. Ninety-eight percent of the people you meet will never meet your parents, check your birth certificate or your possible police record.

Think about yourself. How many clients, associates, or superiors have you taken home, introduced to your wife and family, shown them your home, and then introduced them to your mother and father so that they would see your background and feel secure with your judgments? Think about that.

The truth is we live in a "street culture." When people meet or see you for the first time, they make decisions about you based on that first impression. They rarely, if ever, change those first decisions. You meet most of the people who really count in your life through someone you mutually trust. Business and society make up a huge relay system by which one is made well-known, and through which one gets to know others.

Like it or not, it is that first impression which will dictate future associations—more than performance, more than family, and more than all the time and effort you have spent to be both well-educated and adequate in your chosen profession.

Your business card means almost nothing. What you say may be charming, but it's secondary. Your credibility and, chances are, your lifelong niche with the people in that room were just established by the first impression you made through your appearance. If that first impression wasn't right, you may witness your credibility crumbling, and not understand why. It's more likely that you will miss it entirely, or even ignore it with that sort of vague feeling of discomfort you have when things don't go quite as well as expected.

If you feel this isn't fair—that a person should be judged, not by what he wears but by what kind of person he is and by what he has done with his life, remember this: Life listens only to winners.

Now I know there are some who say they don't care if

their friends drive Cadillacs or live in the right part of town. They're only interested in the human being; in raising wonderful children with beautiful thoughts and ideals. Those are a boy's dreams; we remember those beautiful ideals, but we are talking here about competing in life.

There are also some who insist that they evaluate a man only by his true worth, not by the way he dresses. They get to know him. They observe his conduct and his family and friends. Then they make a rational judgment. I don't believe it. Why? Because if the guy they are talking about was dressed in the iridescent blue shirt, red double-knit pants, or the three-colored shoes with lifts — if he looked like that the first time they met him, chances are they didn't even get his name, much less get to know or understand him.

Certainly most of us have our share of "characters" in our lives, and many are delightful people. However, we don't take their advice and we don't do business with them. We don't dine with them at the country club and we don't include them in our circle of intimates. These characters in our lives are colorful, yes, but they are characters when we first meet them, and they will remain characters always. We don't include them in our computation for success. The philosophy books can idealize man's relationship to his fellow man forever. It's when idealism faces the realities of life that Man, the Survivor, begins to assess what really composes a success quotient. It doesn't take too long to conclude that there is a factor operating in success stories that isn't rational, isn't idealistic, and has largely escaped notice. That factor is the tremendous influence our appearance has on others.

There was a time in all our lives when our appearance mattered most. We had a dream, a dream of success and how to achieve it. We knew without question that the way we looked had a lot to do with the way we succeeded. I'll bet you looked sharp, too.

You understood a great deal about your image, and when it "clicked" you knew it. You wore what was right and it worked.

Perhaps you still know, but most of us have tended to realign our priorities differently from those early years. Our wardrobe gets shuttled down the list of priorities in favor of wife, home, family, car, school, etc. Responsibility.

If your wardrobe has moved down-scale in your priorities, then you need to take a good look now at what success really means to you. If your wardrobe budget gets put aside in favor of a new lawnmower or that weekend trip to the mountains, you may have lost sight of your own purpose in life.

When a man loses sight of his dreams and settles for just keeping up day-to-day, he has also lost sight of a fundamental fact of life. You are either moving forward or you're moving backward. There is no such thing as "just keeping up."

It's not an easy game. It's a tough game, this game of life. Life is like football. You've got your choice. You can sit on the bleachers and bitch. Or you can get down on the field and play. But, if you're going to be on the team, you have to put on the uniform.

This book is for the man who must succeed, who won't settle for less, and who knows that all the stops must be pulled out to succeed.

If you are still unaware or unsure that people read your clothes and put the information away in their subconscious for as long as they remember your name, stop right here. Get out a pad and pencil. Write down the names of ten people you haven't seen in years — schoolmates, college chums, etc. Now, go over your list. One by one you'll see that each name triggered a whole series of visual thoughts, good and bad, about each individual. The pictures roll out as clearly as the first day you saw them. This subconscious of your, that sometimes frightening mechanism of your mind, keeps track of all such data.

Knowing that, it's time you faced up to something. All your friends, all your acquaintances, all your business associates, keep the same or similar facts about you that you keep about them. And knowing *that*, you should make a decision right now that you are not going to spend the rest of your life trying to overcome a bad first impression.

Now, I've heard all the excuses. One gentleman told me, "I'm not in sales. I just sit at a desk, and manage a department. In fact, I only see my boss once a month. My clothes mean nothing. I just try to get a plain suit that'll please my wife." He's right about one thing. The only one who liked that plain suit was his wife because it was on sale. What he obviously doesn't understand is that he is methodically storing a little package of subconscious pictures in his boss' mind once a month. Those pictures and that "plain sale suit" of his only begin to really matter the day the boss is asked to evaluate him for a top management post. What does the boss do?

Does the boss assess dependability, trustworthiness, management skill, and those long years of performance? He automatically takes out the set of subconscious pictures he's been accumulating all these months. In one-tenth of a second he knows. First, he knows that "plain sale suit" just doesn't belong in the company of top executives. Secondly, he knows the executives will be among the first to see that the "plain sale suit" doesn't belong. Thirdly, the boss knows his own executive ability is being subtly examined here, and if he supports old "plain sale suit" then the executives are going to begin to have second thoughts about *his* role in top management.

That's in the first one-tenth of a second. In the second

one-tenth of a second he says "No" to the promotion of one "Plain Sale Suit."

Believe me, no one is ever promoted to an executive position if he would make the other executives uncomfortable by his appearance. Everybody knows a so-called millionaire who is a terrible dresser; don't worry about him. Millionaires are not elevated, they do the elevating. Shabby geniuses are kept in back rooms, out of sight. This book is for the rest of us, trying to get up there.

The moral of this story, if it needs one, is you always dress for where you're going, not for where you are. Dressing for the trip to the top will make getting there that much easier. Remember this about the subconscious mind. It rarely, if ever, wavers from the first impression. Once in a great while, due to unusual circumstances, you meet someone who appears in the double-knit pants, blue iridescent shirt, and two-tone shoes, and he turns out to be a fine friend.

Assume that you meet a man on jury duty and sit together for six weeks. You begin to understand him — the loss of his father when he was very young, the poverty of home, his working to support his mother and young sister. Adversity often produces fine men. All in all, you recognize him as a very special person in his own way, and you like him and respect him for what he has done.

Now jury duty is over. You are out for lunch and bump into one of the senior partners in your firm. You welcome the opportunity to say hello and remind him you are in there pitching. Suddenly, you hear someone call your name. Turning, you see George walking toward you in a plaid-on-plaid double-knit suit, red tie, blue shirt and two-tone platform shoes. Know the feeling? You can see "Why are they friends?" written in capital letters all over the senior partner's face. You will start explaining George and his appearance as soon as he has moved on. Most of us have done it — apologize for a friend's appearance. It's a terrible moment.

Is this to say then that a person cannot succeed if he does not have the "Look"? Must we even choose the friends we make based upon how they are going to look if we have to introduce them to the big boss? Tough, isn't it. But there it is.

Let's compare two men working hard to make the big climb to the top. One corporate climber gets his act together, assembling all the proper climbing equipment, including his education and wardrobe. With planning and determination he will climb his way to the top of the heap and arrive with health and energy to enjoy that great moment of reaching his goal. Another says, "I don't need all that junk." He climbs with great determination and brute strength but without planning and preparation. He encounters setbacks and disappointments at every step. It is as though he had a hundred pound bag of sand on his back. He makes it, yes — but he's exhausted. His health is broken and he's bitter that it has taken all he had. His goal, though reached, seems barren for the price he's paid.

What I want you to see is that this matter of image and dress is not a shallow, vain, and phony effort to please the boss or con someone into thinking you're something you're not. It is a sound preparation for setting an emotional and physical climate for success. It is a business tool and skill. Anyone who would aspire to those lofty heights must know and understand that his health and well-being are wrapped up in his preparations and his effort.

I think it's important to stop right here and say, "There is really no right or wrong way to dress."

You may look up and see a guy in funny clothes, a bum, and a great-looking gentleman walking down the street, and all three of them may be right for themselves at that moment for the roles life has dealt them. If all three of these men walking down the street asked you for the time, which one would you stop and tell? Which one would you walk by and yell at him in passing? Which one would you ignore? Easy, isn't it? Yet, I can't say that any one of them is dressed the wrong way. Let us just say that if you expect anybody to give you the time of day, there is a way to dress for it. You must package yourself for the role you want to play in life.

No one would buy insurance without consulting his insurance man. No one would take medicine without direction from his doctor. Yet the hardest thing in the world to do is tell a good-looking man who is doing well that he is dressing wrong, but if he will change he will do better. It's harder still to get him to accept the advice and act on it.

I have yet to meet a man who did not want to believe that his real value, the one ingredient that put him above all others, was his personality. (In other words, if you get to know me, you'll like me.) But again, this is not how the game of life is played. You must meet and get to know someone to find out about his personality and to appreciate him as person. People just don't get what a great guy you are on first contact. Sometimes, they don't get it until after a long association. Sometimes they never get it. What they get is what your appearance says. They see your clothes long before they even notice the wonderful guy inside them. Before you open your mouth, your clothes start talking for you, up or down, for or against you. It's an integral part of the game. The score card only records whether you won or lost.

Recently one of my customers told me a story that demonstrates this very well. He came from a small town and ran a successful insurance company there until the home office moved him to Atlanta to open a new branch. Several months after setting up the new office, he began to think about his two best buddies back home. There they were—great-looking guys and big producers in spite of their funny clothes. Why? Because back home everyone had gotten to know them and recognized them as trustworthy and dependable. Time had proven their ways. Anyway, after a lot of pull, he got his way and moved them to Atlanta. They were new. Everyone they met judged them by the way they looked. That first impression. They failed because of their clothes. A year later they returned home. Here were two great salesmen who failed because you cannot even give away hundred dollar bills on the street in funny clothes!

Relating the story to me, my friend was very sad. He said, "Bill, I never realized. I loved those two guys and their families. They each had great past performances. I saw only the forest. I never saw the down home way they dressed. I'll never forget that lesson for the rest of my life. I lost two good friends because I judged them with my heart and not my head, where I judge everything else that is important to me."

In all my talks I have always tried above everything else to never hurt anyone's feelings. I was in show business where people were professionals at annihilating feelings. Acting is selling yourself, and as such we were sensitive to every nuance of feeling, to say the least. Mine were crushed enough for all my friends and acquaintances. Consequently, I've been careful how I've explained packaging to people. For example, one day a young man came into my store. We had bought some clothing racks from his company. I was taken by what a nice guy he seemed to be but was skeptical of him because of his dress. So in the course of conversation I turned it around to clothes and was explaining how people read your clothes. To my amazement I hit a tender spot. He turned on me and vehemently explained that he was number one in his territory in what he called the "work sheet," a term obviously used for his amount of productivity. And he repeated over and over with much emotion, "I am number one, number one, you hear me. I've received three raises in two years" . . . and on and on.

There came a moment of silence and I heard myself saying: "Haven't you ever wondered why they haven't taken you off the road and made you an executive?" We sat and looked at each other for a moment. It seemed an eternity. We both sort of laughed and got to talking again. I said, "Pal, do you have a minute?" He looked at me, smiled and nodded his head. I made him take off his wild purple and pink-flowered tie, put on a regimental tie and try on a medium Cambridge gray suit. It was a pretty close fit. I tied his tie in a half-Windsor knot with the dimple right in the center. He had never seen himself look like quality. He found a new person in himself that he liked, and he wanted to see that person again and again. That young man found two friends that day. He began to like and trust me, but more important, he began to like and be proud of himself.

So you see that changing your life through changing appearance is actually very simple. It is one change you can make simply by walking in somewhere and buying something. However, dressing right and packaging yourself is not just money. If it were a matter of money, only the wealthy could dress "right." Making money is usually a big trap. A young man graduates from college, gets a job, finds a wife and has children, which takes— what—ten years before he can breathe? He has hit his first big plateau. For the first time he can go out and buy a new wardrobe without price as his guideline. He looks up, here comes Big Louie, one of the office's big producers. So Louie tells him, "Pal, go out to my store. Look here, my sport coat is the latest fashion, my pants the same. Look at all the pockets. Flaps and needle-stitching all down the side of the pants and coat. First cabin! First cabin, that's the only way I go now. Pick yourself out the alligator shoes and belt to match. Get some white ones for swinging."

Well, he goes and does his thing. So when he walks into an office now the little receptionist with the big, blue eyes says, "Wow, I love your jacket!" (She means, I wish I had one like it, it would look great on me.) However, the client looks at him and in one-tenth of a second makes a number of negative decisions. First, our hard working man, father of three, with a wonderful adoring wife has become a "new boy in town" who has just started making money. Second, he comes from a lower social level with little potential for moving up, and his outfit proves it. Third, education? He probably went into the service instead of finishing high school. What do you think our friend's credibility is at this moment? You know what it is — zero! So you see, it's not just money involved. It's understanding what your clothes say about you and packaging yourself for favorable responses.

Another man came into my store to look around. The salesman showed him where to find his size. He stayed and stayed. Finally, I walked over and said, "Friend, don't feel you're being neglected, you have to ask if you want help." He asked if I were Mr. Thourlby and I said that I was. He began pouring out his story to me, but he spoke listlessly almost as if he were talking about someone else. "I was just told by a friend who is a vice president of our company . . ." he paused, then, "Well, my friend has just read the company's confidential personnel file on me which they keep on all employees, and in essence it said that . . ." pausing again, ". . . that I was number one in sales but my appearance was an embarrassment to the company at every big sales meeting, and it was hard to tell what effect my appearance had on the personal sales relationships developed in representing the firm." Watching his eyes as he related the story I could see and feel the pain. It was a cry for help from a great big, fine-looking man who had been wounded to the core and was hurting.

Quietly I asked, "When is the next sales meeting?" He hesitated, sighed and said, "I have to leave for Kansas City on Sunday for the national conference." "This is Thursday," I said, "Let's get started." We packaged him in two suits with several shirt and tie combinations all saying the right things. Trying them on, Saturday, he shed his old look forever and became a giant in the process, until I looked at his shoes. "Pal, the shoes gotta go too." I picked out a pair of simple smooth-toed black shoes. We then traded his red and green plastic suit bag for an inexpensive canvas travel bag. I told him, "When you arrive, do not, *do not* tell anyone you have talked to me or changed anything. Just play this and enjoy yourself. When someone says he likes this or that, just thank him and do not go into it. Act just like this is the way it has always been and drop by and let me know how it went." I did not see him for three weeks, but he sent me a card saying, "Today is the first day of my life." Later he enjoyed telling me that when he walked in to register he was met with silence—stunned silence. He said "Bill, I never said a word. I was thrilled and enjoyed every second."

He told me a story I'll share with you because it illustrates a good point. He said, "Bill, Sunday night I phoned my wife and told her all about what had happened. She had seen my clothes and knew what I was doing. I said, 'Honey, I'm really proud of myself tonight, and all my life I've wanted you to be proud of me.' She told me, 'Darling, I've always been proud of you. I just want the rest of the world to get to know you as I do.' That moment," he said, "I fell in love with my wife all over again." Did he go back to his customers and overpower them? Of course not. When you begin to dress with a conservative, quality look, your business associates, your clients, and your friends will all understand what that look represents. Dressing right is the secret for developing poise and confidence in business.

Another thing, don't make the mistake of "dressing down" to a client. His old work clothes may feel and look fine on him, but if you showed up in something similar he'd say you looked funny—or worse, phony. Even if you have to visit a farm or work site to see your client and he is wearing work clothes it's a simple thing to slip off the jacket, loosen the tie, and turn up the cuffs twice. You'll put him at ease. But make no mistake. He knows plenty of lawyers, insurance men, and salesmen who wear all the funny clothes. If dressing down would convince him, they would already have his business. Your simple relaxing gesture communicates yet retains your image and allows your clothes to keep on saying "I'm competent, I'm professional, and you can trust me."

Why do professionals spend so much money on their reception rooms? They do it because they know when you are seeking help in their field, be it medicine, accounting, sales, insurance, or anything else, you seek the best. You want the office to look right and the man who runs it to look right. Professionals control the impression they present very carefully, so that you make the correct judgments about their credibility, trustworthiness, and knowledgeability.

When you need serious consultation, you will invariably seek a man at an equal or higher level than your own. No short cuts. You want the best and you'll look till you get it.

Let me relate another example of how packaging yourself through your appearance can change your life. One morning at breakfast in my favorite restaurant, I heard someone say, "Good morning, Bill." Looking up I recognized a man I saw only occasionally. He said, "Mind if I join you?" We sat over coffee and small-talked. Suddenly he said, "Bill, I remember all you said at that talk you gave to our business club. Things are going well for me and I want to ask you a question." As I sat there, all I could see was double-knit plaid. It reminded me of a field of rhubarb. He had on a white shirt with airplanes all over it and a funny tie, so busy I cannot remember it. Of course, I knew what question he was set to ask. It always embarrasses me to be asked a loaded question.

"Now, honestly, Bill, what do you think of my outfit?" There it was. Well, maybe it was the time of day or the Irish in me, but I went right on eating and said, "Well, with all the good Lord gave you, to package it in that outfit, you should have your you-know-what kicked." At that, there was a long silence. I wished I had continued eating instead of talking. Finally, he said, "What time does your store open? I'll see you there." About an hour later he came in and we talked some more, laughing about my little remark. Then he said, "All right, Bill, you pick out a suit, a shirt and a tie. I'm going to let you do it and I'm not going to say a word."

He picked up his suit a few days later, saying how much he really liked it. It was about ten days before he appeared in the store again. We were busy. He stayed until I finally got over to him, and I asked him if he would like coffee. Immediately, he said, "How much is that suit worth?" pointing to his new suit. I figured he must have seen the same suit somewhere else on sale and now wanted a ten dollar rebate. So I said, "That suit is worth exactly what value you put on it, no more and no less." He smiled, and said, "Well then, it's worth eighteen thousand dollars." I stood awed by such a statement, but I sold him the suit so I was not about to argue. He unraveled his story about the one account he'd been after for four years. He told me how he had packaged himself with the calculated-response suit, shirt, and tie and went to see his prospective client.

"When I walked in, everything changed," he said. "I had taken command. I set the goals and how we could get them done. To my amazement I heard my client say, 'All right, but I'm only signing for six months, not five years.' I found myself saying, 'Mr. Anderson, you want a quality job, and you want it done right? Sign for five years.' My client smiled and said okay. I was stunned. I could not get my feet to move. For four years straight this man would not even discuss details and all of a sudden, he's insisting. So, that's why the suit is worth eighteen thousand dollars to me."

Finally, a special word about minorities. Reading and analyzing this book should make you realize that we are all minorities of one when it comes to managing the impression we make. We either package ourselves to achieve the desired effect from others, or we don't, regardless of the color of our skin or our nationality. Anyone in a funny suit is still someone in a funny suit. In business, the only real color that counts or that the world is interested in is "green," as in greenbacks. Consequently, the same guidelines in packaging for the businessman apply to everyone.

Equality is a reality, backed by the power of the United States government. Opportunity exists for everyone. Yet those opportunities will be taken by those who use their appearance to say that they are capable and deserving of the responsibilities each opportunity offers, regardless of their race or nationality. "Roots" are not as important today as ability. Companies today buy brains, not background. The future is now for people who can produce. One way you, as a member of a "minority," can get the opportunity to produce is to have your appearance help you rather than hinder you. As the Queen of England wrote to her son, the Prince of Wales, "Dress gives one the outward sign from which people in general can and often do judge upon the inward state of mind and feelings of a person; for this they can see; while the other they cannot see. On that account clothes are of particular importance, particularly for a person of high rank."

If clothes and what they say about one are that important to the Queen of England, who obviously cannot rise much higher, how important can they be to those of us who are reaching for opportunity. Use your appearance to get you up to bat. After that the rules are the same for everyone, and you are ready to move into the next minority—the one that owns and runs this country.

For all, nothing succeeds like success.

> *"The world is governed more by appear-*
> *ance than by realities, so that it is fully*
> *as necessary to seem to know something*
> *as it is to know it."*
>
> —Daniel Webster

2

CIRCUMSTANTIAL EVIDENCE IS ENOUGH

A basic tenet of law holds that a person can be convicted purely on circumstantial evidence. And the people we meet every day immediately judge us on the circumstantial evidence of our clothing and appearance. They determine how to behave toward us, whether or not to trust us and how they think we will behave toward them almost entirely on how we are dressed and appear to them. The first impression we make on others is of crucial importance in our success in dealing with our fellow human beings, whether it be in the business, social, or even the religious world. We, in turn, form instantaneous opinions of those we meet, based on their appearance, which influence the way we will behave toward them. One of the main reasons we instantly judge people is that we are survivors in a harsh, cruel world. We must immediately decide if this particular person will be either beneficial or harmful to our future, family, or finances. When it comes to these areas of our life, and since everyone we come in contact with will affect one of them, we immediately size them up so that we know how to deal with them.

As survivors, we quickly form a first impression of everyone we meet. We read a person's clothing, appearance, and other nonverbal cues as sort of a silent language or visual shorthand which gives us subjective decisions about the other fellow's honesty, background, friendliness, attitudes, and intent with regard to our well-being. If you don't think this is true, visualize for a minute walking down a dark alleyway and meeting in turn a white-haired gentleman carrying a briefcase, dressed in a suit, tie and white shirt, a policeman dressed in his uniform, and then a member of the Hell's Angels motorcycle gang decked out in his warring colors. Although the contrasts are overstated, the point is certainly made: In order to survive you immediately size up the individual to determine your course of behavior toward him. We do the same thing to everyone we meet, although on a subtler and more subconscious level. We form a lasting first impression of those we come in contact with which influences our subsequent behavior toward them.

Psychologists tell us that forming a first impression is similar to peeling an onion. We scan the surface qualities of the other individual immediately and, if time permits, we later look for deeper qualities. Unfortunately, the hectic pace of life today seldom affords us the leisure to look for these qualities in people we meet. Consequently, we are forced to develop criteria upon which to judge those we meet. Clothing and appearance can be considered one of the most important (if not the premium) measurements we use. The need for such criteria is readily apparent. The degree to which we are successful as survivors in life depends upon our ability to understand and predict other people's behavior. If people were constantly surprising us life would be intolerable.

Consider, if you will, a life suddenly turned topsy-turvy, wherein people dressed as priests and ministers suddenly became rapists and muggers. Or policemen in their uniforms symbolizing authority, order and protection, suddenly behaved as frightened children. Again, the analogy illustrates the need for criteria on which to predict and understand other people's behavior.

These criteria are based on our private development of philosophies of human nature and identification of role stereotypes. Our philosophies of human nature are simply assumptions on our part that everyone has certain qualities to a degree and that if we can identify that degree in someone's appearance, the chances are that he will behave a certain way. Consequently, if a person's clothing gives us the impression that he comes from a good background and is honest, we assume that he will behave a certain way. The reverse is also true.

In addition to these philosophies of human nature, we base our criteria for instant judgment of others on the identification of role stereotypes. Everyone possesses some stereotypes of simplified images of certain groups of people. For example, most of us expect doctors to be warm, knowledgeable people experienced in medicine, who can help us when we are sick. Therefore, when we see someone dressed in a doctor's uniform wearing a stethoscope around his neck, we make these same assumptions about this individual.

Since our clothing covers up 90 percent of our bodies and dominates our appearance, it's not hard to see what an important part our clothing is in the criteria by which we form our first impressions of others. Likewise, others perceive us in terms of our clothing and appearance, using their preconceived notions or philosophies of human nature and role identification to immediately judge us. They attribute to us certain qualities, favorable or unfavorable, based upon our clothing and appearance, and behave toward us accordingly.

Although as survivors we are all adept at applying these criteria of clothing and appearance to others, we seldom turn the coin around and study what our own clothes say about us to those we meet. We quickly size up and judge others based on their clothing and appearance but give little heed to what we broadcast to others with our own appearance. In fact, the messages broadcast by others are often easier to perceive and recognize than our own. In addition, we neglect a very important part of life since first impressions are largely derived from outward appearances, and the way in which we are first perceived is particularly important in establishing ourselves in new social roles.

The importance of this concept cannot be overlooked. Essentially, we can package ourselves in such a way that we can predict how others will perceive us and thus structure our own role in a given situation. In plain language, we can use our appearance to determine how those we meet will react toward us and thus control our own role in this situation. We, in effect, control the impression that we give others for a specific reason, namely to control their behavior toward us. This controlling of impressions we present to others is called Impression Management by psychologists.

Impression management refers to all those strategies and techniques used by individuals to control the images and impressions that others form of them during social interaction. In order to successfully perform impression management, individuals must know what behaviors on their part will create what impressions in the eyes and minds of their beholder. They must be skilled at taking the role of others and able to convincingly and naturally perform precisely those verbal and nonverbal acts that will create the desired image. *

In the next chapter we will explore how we can manage impressions through packaging ourselves to influence and

* From Laurence S. Wrightman, Social Psychology, (Belmont, Calif., Wadsworth Publishing Company, Inc., 1972), p. 143.

manipulate the behavior of others.

3

IMPRESSION MANAGEMENT THROUGH PACKAGING

Clothing has long served the purpose as a symbol of the role or status an individual enjoys in his particular society, obtaining for him the rewards of recognition, approval, and identification. Early clothing symbols can be traced back to Paleolithic times when the hunter adorned himself with the skin or bones of an animal he killed to broadcast his achievement. Down through the ages chiefs and leaders adopted certain articles of clothing to identify themselves to friend and foe alike. Crowns, headdresses, and unique clothing forms were reserved for wear by persons of exalted status in every society. Ecclesiastical hierarchy can be observed in the clothing habits of popes, bishops, and other officials of the medieval church. Even today, such easily identifiable symbols of rank and status can be seen in the uniforms of the armed forces. Such clear-cut manifestations of clothing as a symbol of status and rank are perfect examples of impression management through clothing in an attempt to influence the behavior of others. Certain articles of clothing indicated (and still do) rank and authority, and consequently the behavior of those to which this image was recognizable was influenced. In fact, this impression management through clothing was often implemented through the use of sumptuary laws.

Sumptuary laws are laws which are passed to prohibit the wearing of certain types of clothing by certain types of individuals within a society. Many good examples of such laws are found in the feudal societies of Europe. As class and station in life became solidified, certain forms of clothing became identified with the ruling nobles. The wide discrepancy of dress between nobles and peasants, in fact, reflected the widely held notion that every man was born to a station in life. The clothing worn by the ruling classes was a form of impression management which identified the wearer as a nobleman and someone to be obeyed and treated with deference. With the rise of the wealthy merchant class, the nobles passed laws which restricted the clothing the merchants could purchase with their wealth. This was an attempt to maintain their class identity and implement impression management through legal means.

Today the importance of clothing's use to manipulate behavior is seen in the attempts of socialistic and totalitarian societies to eradicate class distinctions by requiring all citizens to wear similar dress. The important point to be understood from history is that impression management through the use of clothing is nothing new. It has been employed effectively since the beginning of time.

Two things of tremendous impact have occurred in recent times which have made the concept of impression management through clothing of such importance to everyone. The first is the complete changing of the American life style since the end of the second world war. America is no longer a nation of rural communities or sharply defined neighborhoods where everyone had a well known and easily recognizable identity. People seldom work in the same community in which they live. Their business contacts are with virtual strangers. They hardly know the people they work alongside of all day. They live in beehives of apartment houses or sprawling subdivisions, little knowing or caring who their neighbors are. One's life is a series of encounters with people he hardly knows or knows not at all. Consequently, we live our lives continually sizing up and instantaneously judging strangers we live and work with by their clothing and appearance, which are the only criteria available. Therefore, if we choose, we can determine the outcome of these encounters by influencing the behavior of these strangers we meet through managing the impression we make on them by using our clothing we wear to package ourselves for a predictable response. In effect, to those we meet in everyday life, we are what we wear.

The second important change which has made the power of clothing and its use so critical is the appearance of television and its pervasive influence on everyone's life, especially with regard to how we perceive our fellow human beings. Television has broken the boundaries of our perception and shown us our leaders—the wealthy, the powerful, the charismatic, and the successful. More importantly, it has shown us what they look like. In addition, it has shown the less fortunate of our society—the poor, the criminal, the ill, and anarchic. It has also shown what they look like. Television not only serves the function of helping to form stereotypes of certain groups, it reinforces these stereotypes continually. We see how certain people are dressed as well as having them minutely analyzed and interpreted for us. We develop philosophies of human nature by which we impart to these people the qualities which television tells us to expect. If we see someone who looks like a successful executive shown on television, then we instantly assume that is what he is. If we see someone who looks like he is a pimp on TV, then we instantly assume that he is a pimp.

The shaping of the criteria by which we judge others is not limited to television showing us what certain groups of people look like. Network programming consists almost entirely of morality plays in which we identify people by the way they are dressed. Actors are carefully packaged by wardrobe departments to tell the audience through their clothing and appearance what the character of their role is. When such subjective judgments are borne out in the course of the play, the development of clothing as a criterion of judgment is reinforced. Thus, television has the awesome power of shaping how man looks at his contemporaries by influencing, if not outright controlling, the criteria by which he judges them.

In brief, the consequences of these two great changes are that essentially no one really knows who anyone is, and television shapes and influences the criteria we use to judge those we meet. We can use these two factors to package ourselves so that people accept us at face value by wearing clothing and structuring our appearance to coincide with the preconceived notions which are implanted and amplified in people by the influence of the media. For example, if we should decide that it is to our advantage to look like a successful businessman in a given situation, then we can simply package ourselves to look like one. Almost everyone we meet will think that is exactly what we are. The key to successfully using impression management is understanding how others perceive us. Our own opinion of the way others see us is often faulty. The purpose of this book is to help you understand how other people see and judge you based on the clothing and appearance you present. It is up to you to take the necessary steps to package yourself so that people then see you the way you want them to.

In general, it is safe to say that people like people who are basically similar to themselves, hold the same ideas and values, and act in approximately the same ways. Therefore, if you would use your appearance to make people like you, you would package yourself to be similar to those people you wish to have like you. However, for business purposes it is not necessary that you be liked. You must package yourself to fit the preconceived notion that is necessary to influence the behavior of others in a business situation. For example, to sell life insurance to an individual it is more important to be credible, trustworthy, and knowledgeable than to be likable. Therefore, you plan your appearance so that you look like what his preconceived notion of a successful insurance agent is. If you package yourself to be credible, trustworthy, and knowledgeable, he will like you. On the other hand, you can use impression management to maintain social distance. Simply plan your appearance to be completely dissimilar from the individual in question and to be a stereotype of the type of person this particular individual would abhor. The main emphasis is on understanding what your clothing says about you and people in general. We will analyze what specific articles of clothing say to the world in general. You must then take these ingredients and package yourself to achieve your own goals—whatever they may be. Should your goal be success in business, you will package yourself one way. Should something else be more important to you at this stage of your life then you will learn how to package yourself accordingly. The decision is yours.

Before we get into specifics of what your clothes say about you, we must explore a very dramatic and exciting consequence of managing the impression you present to others by planning and packaging yourself through your clothing and appearance. As we have pointed out, to those you meet, you are what you wear. However, the fantastic thing that can change your life dramatically is that, to yourself, you can become what you wear.

Appearances are of four kinds. Things either are what they appear to be, or they neither are nor appear to be; or they are, and do not appear to be; or they are not, and yet appear to be.

Samuel Johnson

4

Power Through Packaging

Each year twenty-five billion dollars are spent by American industry to present their products to the public in attractive, appealing, familiar and reassuring packages. Millions of dollars are spent developing packaging (90 percent of which is discarded upon use) that says the right things about such mundane items as soap, toothpaste, and cigarettes. The psychology of packaging embraces color appeal, container silhouette, and product description. In addition to the product, the company image is packaged through the use of company logos, business cards, stationery, and media advertising. Yet the packaging of the single most important product and image setter industry has, the businessman, is neglected and abused.

By understanding impression management through appearance you can begin to plan your appearance and package yourself to generate an automatic positive response from those you meet in business and social situations. In simple terms, give the other fellow what you think he wants. You instinctively employ impression management already through tone of voice and facial expression.

In packaging yourself, you must first consider the fact that your appearance immediately initiates ten decisions in the first impression you make on others.

1. Economic level
2. Educational level
3. Trustworthiness
4. Social position
5. Sophistication
6. Economic heritage
7. Social heritage
8. Educational heritage
9. Success in chosen field
10. Moral character

Now you can study certain situations to determine how you can use your appearance to influence whoever you're dealing with. Let's take the job interview.

Interview

When interviewed recently, the president of the world's largest employment agency, stated, "The most important thing in getting a job is appearance and personality. Skill and something to back it up with is second. Skill is important, but it is second." And he went on to explain that what he meant by appearance was simply the way a person dressed. Looking at the chart above you can see that although all the decisions are important, your appearance should especially tell the interviewer that you're trustworthy (3), well educated (2), successful (9), or about to be, and have good moral character (10).

In addition, to develop a successful interview wardrobe, you analyze the industry and company you're interested in working in. Lawyers and salesmen dress differently. Also, each company within an industry has its image from conservative to flamboyant. After considering these two factors, lean toward the conservative side both for the industry and within the company.

Finally, the purpose of the interview is to get the job offer, not impress the interviewer, make a date with his secretary, or turn heads on the street. Therefore, make sure your outfit is low keyed, so that the man across the desk can concentrate on you, not your flashy pinkie ring, your hand painted tie, or your plastic shoes.

The Fail-Safe Interview Outfit

After thinking about the above factors you can develop a fail-safe interview outfit that says all the right things about you. Wear a medium to dark gray natural shoulder suit, white shirt, and regimental striped tie. The medium- to dark-gray is a likable yet serious color. The natural shoulder indicates that you are traditional, conservative, hence dependable and responsible. The white shirt, with either button-down collar or straight points reinforces the impression of straightforwardness and trustworthiness, while the regimental tie suggests a back ground of good education; i.e., the Ivy League.

Wear black, lace-up shoes, either wing tip or plain-toed. Black is a powerful authoritative color, while the lace-up conveys a picture of dependability since you obviously take more time to get dressed than simply slipping on a pair of loafers. Forget the school ring, you've already said that you're well educated. If married, wear a small plain wedding band. Anything else is overdone.

Wear black over the calf socks. Nothing robs you of credibility more than the sight of your bare leg when you cross your legs. Try it in the mirror.

Complete your picture of the well-educated, successful, and dependable individual by carrying a plain black or brown leather briefcase devoid of combination or ornate locks. The leather indicates quality; you obviously can afford the better things in life, therefore you are successful or about to be. A plastic briefcase says all the wrong things about you, in addition to suggesting that you would skimp on the important things in order to save a few dollars. Combination locks or ornate locks not only are in poor taste, but suggest that you're in the habit of leaving your briefcase somewhere or that you're got something to hide. Both impressions hurt your credibility and trustworthiness.

On the second interview, you've gotten past the personnel man and are likely to meet the person you'll work for. Most line managers have little regard for the personnel department. They consider themselves the money makers, while personnel is simply a staff function that spends money, often foolishly in the line managers' view. Whether or not this is true, the plain facts indicate that line managers hire who they like regardless of what personnel says. For this reason, on the second interview wear a darker, more authoritative suit. A white shirt and dressier tie will give you a stronger, controlled aggressive air. This is important to the people who make the profit and loss decision. Complete your outfit as you did for the first interview so that your appearance says you're knowledgeable, trustworthy, well educated, and successful. Remember when you walk into the interview your appearance instantly says more about you than your resume, your past job history, and hours of conversation in the interview. The man usually makes up his mind to hire you or not as you come in the door.

Think about what you want your appearance to say. You'll get up to bat more often and consequently score more runs. By now you should have the hang of it, but let's briefly look at some more situations where you can use your appearance to win.

On the Job

Although they don't say it, most managers when pressed agree that "you never get promoted to a position you don't look like you belong in." Understanding this can help you realize you dress for the position you want, not the one you're in. In other words, dress for where you're going, not where you're at. Think about what you want your appearance to say to your contemporaries and higher management.

Again, although the way you package yourself should instantly evoke positive responses in all ten areas, on the job you should look successful and competent. Fortunately, that's easy to accomplish with a little common sense. First, separate your contemporaries into categories based on the way they dress. It's also not hard to identify which ones are on the way up, have been pigeon-holed, or are on the way down.

You emulate but not parrot the men on the move in your company. Follow the lead of the more conservatively dressed men who are moving up. Fast Eddie may sell a lot out in the field in his high fashion designer suit with the funny shirts and ties and tri-colored shoes, but he certainly would not be invited into the board room for serious discussions. Unfortunately, that's all Eddie will ever be — a salesman — because that's what he looks like.

In addition, you'll be taken more seriously in darker suits. If you went into the office wearing a white suit, looking like the Kentucky Colonel, you'll have trouble making anyone really listen to what you have to say. If you have to take your suit jacket off in the office, you're right that rolling up your sleeves will give the impression that you're working hard. But be careful to only roll them up twice on the outside. If you roll them up further you'll look like you belong on the loading dock, not where the decision makers are. If you roll them up on the inside you have a slightly shifty air, like a gambler or a con man. If you walk into the office and the receptionist tells you that you have a beautiful tie on, it's probably not right for you. What she's really saying is she thinks the colors and materials would look beautiful on her.

Take a little more time in the morning to look at yourself in a full-length mirror to see if you have packaged yourself to accomplish what you want that day. An added hint is to periodically wash your hands and face during the day. This will give you a fresh, scrubbed, alert look that makes people think you handle your affairs in a brisk, competent manner. Simply analyze what you want to be, and then dress that way.

Dress to Intimidate

How about dressing to intimidate or dominate those people who often cause some of your most frustrating moments in everyday life? For example, how about planning your appearance to bowl over that snooty headwaiter or hostess who keeps you waiting forever for a table in a restaurant. What about getting that slow motion clerk in the local post office or store to listen to what you want and then do it. How about dressing to help you get that loan that you really need from the loan officer who's got the money, but it going to make you crawl to get it. Robert Ringer in his book *Winning Through Intimidation* adopted the black business suit, black horn rimmed glasses, and black briefcase for an image picture to intimidate. It certainly worked for him.

It is not that simple, but by using your chart you can structure your appearance to handle these situations. The headwaiter, clerk, or loan officer takes one look at you and decides exactly how he is going to treat you. You'd better be sure that your appearance says the right things about you in that decisive moment. For the headwaiter, everything about you should say that you are used to the finer things in life, expect, even demand good service, and can afford to pay for it. You should look important enough so that he should want to seat you promptly so that you are seen. You exemplify the type of clientele he wants in his establishment. You can accomplish this by using the chart again to highlight your social position, economic level, and sophistication. In general, follow a couple of simple rules. In the more expensive restaurants, the darker, more dominant suit is required. Wear dark blue, charcoal, or black suits. For even more exclusive restaurants and clubs, wear a dark suit with a pin stripe or chalk stripe. Wear expensive black lace-up shoes, either wing-tip or plain toe. Your entire appearance and manner should broadcast simple, expensive elegance. The loud, double- knit suit in funny colors makes you look like some rube dressed up for his one night on the town in the big city,and you'll be treated as such.

Remember, the dressier your appearance, the more you'll look like you routinely dine well and elegantly. For example, wear a solid gray silk tie, white shirt and either gray or white pocket handkerchief. This conveys an impression of sophistication and savoir faire. You can never be overdressed for dining out but you certainly can be underdressed. Walk into a nice restaurant dressed like the average individual and you'll be given average service. Look like you and your family have had money since day one and you'll be treated accordingly.

Planning your appearance to deal with clerks and service people is easy if you again consider the above chart. Obviously you want to command respect from this individual, so you simply dress like people in his life who represent authority to him. His boss, his father, his minister, his school principal, and all those others who have told him what to do all his life, have dressed a certain way, usually in a dark suit. A clerk will wield his limited powers of annoyance and frustration over those whom he considers to be his equals or less fortunate. Simply present him with an appearance of austere affluence. Look like those who have been in control of his life and he'll knuckle under quickly. Try to deal with him dressed in your hippie weekend outfit, and he'll put you through your paces.

Planning your appearance for the loan officer is a little more complicated. It's a generally accepted banking principle that you never lend money to anyone who needs it. The reasoning is simple—the borrower must be able to pay it back. A further consideration is that the lending officer keeps his job by making good loans. Too many defaults and he's out of a job. Therefore, your appearance must stress your good economic background, position, success quotient, and moral character. In addition, you must appear friendly and trustworthy; consequently, you should dress somewhat like you would for the job interview, yet slightly relaxed and friendlier. You achieve this friendlier, relaxed image by wearing a light gray or beige suit. Wear slip-on loafers and black socks. Maintain the impression of economic heritage with the regimental tie or the silk foulard Ivy League tie. Avoid colors and fabrics that smack of working class or new money attitudes, such as purples, black raincoats, or light pastel suits. Don't try to overpower him with the dominant colors, such a dark blue or charcoal gray, because you are, after all, there to ask for something from him. You should look relaxed and confident. Carry a briefcase and a gold pen and pencil to indicate you mean business. Above all, remember to convey an impression that you really don't need the money, and chances are pretty good you'll get it.

Attracting Women

Planning your appearance to attract women is similar to planning a battle campaign. You must identify the enemy. What type of woman are you interested in? Study the battlefield—the social occasion where you'll meet them, and determine your strategic goals—a one-night stand or a longer relationship. In general, most women can be thought to want security which is easily related to economic background, economic level, and success level on our chart. However, in certain situations, such as the single bar, vacation cruise, or unstructured parties, excitement and the possibility of sexual gratification become important to the woman. Consequently, you package yourself according to your goals and the goals of the woman in question.

For example, at the singles bar, wear tightly tailored high fashion suits, tricky color combinations, and more expensive jewelry. The jewelry should still be simple and tasteful, yet obviously expensive. In informal situations wear body shirts and hip-hugging slacks, as women also like to "man watch." Dress with a slightly arrogant air, as this will convey an air of excitement and anger which is attractive to the woman in this situation. She's probably looking for the same thing you are.

In situations where you are looking for a more serious relationship, go back to the classic, traditional look, which conveys good background and economic strength. In more informal situations, such as the cocktail party, wear dark dominating suits which suggest power and security, yet slightly overdress to develop excitement and arrogance. In more informal situations, wear blazers, buttoned-down shirts, and gray or tan slacks. Suggest an appearance of old money and stability, yet open the shirt collar or wear trickier tie and shirt combinations to show that you are not staid but simply more sure of yourself than the fellow in the designer suit who needs the designer's name to tell the world that he's with it. Remember, you can dress to attract the girl you'd like to bring home to Mom, or for a casual evening. It all depends on how you package yourself.

I've covered these specific situations so that you may get a feel for how to package yourself. As you've seen, the key is to analyze the situation you'll be in and determine what things must be emphasized in your appearance.

Willy was a salesman. And for a salesman, there is no rock bottom to the life. He don't put a bolt to a nut, he don't tell you the law or give you medicine. He's a man way out there in the blue, riding on a smile and a shoeshine. And when they start not smiling back— that's an earthquake. And then you get yourself a couple of spots on your hat, and you're finished. Nobody doesn't blame this man. A salesman is got to dream, boy. It comes with the territory.
—Arthur Miller, *Death of a Salesman*

5

PACKAGE THE IMPRESSION

There are three important factors which influence the packaging you can use to help you sell. They are your product, client mix, and your territory or geographical location. You must understand that the way you package yourself has a direct bearing on the success you will have selling yourself, your ideas, or your product or service. If you want to be successful in selling, then package yourself so that your appearance begins to close the deal before you even open your mouth.

Let's see how these factors influence your appearance packaging.

Whatever your product is, take the time to analyze how it affects your packaging, and then begin to plan your wardrobe accordingly.

First, the product has a very important influence on the role the direct salesman should play. Is it a tangible or intangible product? Is it a big ticket or low cost? Is it for homeowners or industrial users? The answers to these questions are very important to the salesman's packaging of himself. In general, the more directly a product influences the customer's money, future, or family, the more serious a role the salesman must present. For example, insurance, securities, and health care require that the salesman package himself by dressing in clothes which are serious in nature — suits, dark ties, and white or blue shirts. Luxury items, recreational products, and novelty products allow the salesman to package himself more casually — sport coats, slacks, and less formal ties.

The second important influence on the role portrayed by the direct salesman is his client mix. What type of customer does he call on? The educational background, social standing, and economic level of the prospect or customer should help the salesman determine what type of appearance he should present to successfully manage the impression he conveys to the customer for judgment. For example, should your customers predominantly be wealthy homeowners, you should package yourself so that your appearance says that you come from a similar background. If your appearance suggests that you come from a lower economic background you will have little chance of being accepted and trusted by this type of client. Similarly, if you call on highly educated prospects such as engineers or professional people, your appearance should suggest a similar background. You can accomplish this by wearing regimental ties, traditional, conservative suits, and solid button-down shirts. Again, whatever your client mix is, take the time to analyze their educational backgrounds, economic levels, and social standings to package yourself accordingly.

Finally, the territory or geographical location will affect the image the successful salesman should present to the customer. The old adage "When in Rome, do as the Romans do" doesn't apply to traveling salesmen. You should be consistent in your appearance whether you're in Florida one day and California the next.

Traditional, quality clothing is acceptable anywhere. Although you shouldn't change your image by dressing like the natives, you should remember that some areas of the country are more formal than others. For example, the East Coast is characterized by more formality in business dress than certain parts of the South or the West Coast. Therefore, your appearance should vary in formality depending on where you are. Analyze the geographical area with regard to formality or informality in business and dress accordingly. If you begin to study these factors and apply impression management to your selling by dressing yourself for your sales role as a wardrobe designer would, you'll begin to notice that although it won't make you a better closer, this approach will get you to bat more often by making you credible to your customer or prospect. As you package yourself to say all the right things to your clients with your appearance and dress, you'll find yourself more readily accepted. Think about it. If your client accepts you fully, he'll begin to consider you a friend rather than just a salesman. He'll start to invite you home to meet his family and friends. You'll never be invited anywhere if you wear the kind of clothes that would embarrass your client in front of his family or associates.

Here as a few general principles to follow in packaging yourself to let your appearance help you sell:

1. Never wear double-knit suits, sport coats, pants, or shirts. Double-knit material has an unmistakably inexpensive look, which says all the wrong things about a salesman.

2. Wear darker clothing for more serious selling situations. Suits, in fact, can be rated on a scale of one to ten. The dark blue suit or charcoal gray suit may be considered as ten, while the all-white Kentucky Colonel suit can be considered a one. The more serious the selling situation, then the more serious the suit. Remember, lighter colors, although friendlier and not as intimidating, must be reserved for less serious sales calls.

3. Sport coats can be worn in less formal selling occupations such as selling door-to-door or cold calling, but they should be recognizable as traditional, quality clothing which says the right things about you to your prospect.

4. Make sure all your accessories such as watches and jewelry are simple and tasteful. Gaudy, flashy accessories give you a distrustful and shifty air similar to the proverbial Honest-John used-car salesman.

5. Wear dark brown or black shoes for business. Anything else is too flashy and destroys your credibility. In addition, wear black over the calf socks to avoid showing your legs when you cross them.

6. Avoid high fashion and exaggerated styles of clothing. These constantly changing fashion swings suggest instability, immaturity, and undependability to your customer or prospect.

Take these basic concepts and begin to think about how to package yourself for more success in your chosen selling field. Remember first that people you meet judge you by your appearance. Second, since your clothes cover up 90 percent of your body, they dominate your appearance. Consequently, they provide most of the material with which people instantly judge you. Third, consider the concept of impression management by packaging yourself to control the image you present to people so that you can predict their response to you. Fourth, remember and think about how you would package yourself if you were a wardrobe designer dressing yourself for the role of a successful salesman in your field. Finally, consider the interesting implications of this thought. If you package yourself as a successful salesman in your field by dressing the way such an individual would, wearing only those clothes which say the right things about you to the people you meet, your customers, prospects, and friends alike will begin to treat you as such. They will respond to the image you present in a predictable way by buying your product, your ideas, or yourself, in other words, look successful and you will become successful.

6

YOU CAN BECOME WHAT YOU WEAR

Right now you're probably thinking "If it were only true. Is it possible that I can change my life by simply changing the way I dress? Can I become happier, more successful, and even more financially secure merely by wearing different clothing and changing the way I appear to others?" Before you dismiss the concept as impossible, a careful analysis needs to be given to the way clothing and appearance helps shape our personalities and how we see ourselves.

Consciously or unconsciously, the clothing we wear reveals a set of beliefs about ourselves that we want the world to believe. In addition, the clothing we choose for ourselves expresses what we believe to be important. For example, many of us express our social values by the clothes we wear. The hippie mode of dress expressed a sense of freedom along with the rejection of more traditional values prevalent in our society. The hippie appearance became a uniform-like way of announcing to the world at large as well as to the wearer himself what he was and how he felt about society and life in general.

Consider for a moment the fact that every significant change in life requires a change in the clothing we wear. Birth, illness, and even death require a specialized change of clothing. The conscious decisions we make which alter our lives all require a codified change of dress or uniform. When we go off to school we wear a certain type of clothing. When we get married we wear another specialized set of clothing. When we graduate from school we don the robes of academia to accept our diploma. In fact, every significant change of situation in life requires a change of dress or clothing. This alteration of appearance indicates to the world and ourselves what the new situation is and helps to define it. For instance, should we join the army, the first radical change we undergo is the shearing of our locks and the donning of the uniform. This can sometimes be a rather brutal and abrupt definition of one's new situation, and is psychologically planned as the first step in "remaking the man" or making a soldier out of him.

Actually the effect clothing and appearance has on the development of personality and the way we see ourselves runs much deeper than these rather obvious examples. Our appearance is a dominant factor in the development of personality in every stage of life. From the moment of birth we are almost never without clothing. In fact, in the very early stages of life we cannot distinguish between our bodies and our clothing. As we explore our bodies and study our fingers and toes, we consider our clothing to be part of us. Gradually our clothing begins to shape and color the way we look at ourselves. We distinguish our sex through our clothing. Baby boys are dressed in blue and baby girls in pink. Later, our clothing serves to separate us into the sex roles we assume. One way we recognize that we are boys and girls is that we dress a certain way. Clothing helps us identify with members of our own sex. Eventually, the actual selection of our clothing begins to satisfy some of our basic needs such as autonomy, attention, individuality, and sex and peer group identification. In addition, our clothing and appearance aid in the step by step growth of personality and self-concept by determining the roles we play, and through presenting ourselves for approval to those who are important in our lives.

This role theory suggests that we present different roles to those who are significant in our lives. If a particular role meets with approval and is rewarded by a favorable response, that role becomes a part of our behavior. Gradually these rewarded roles come together and begin to form personality and self-concept. Clothing and appearance are a very important part of these roles we present and help shape the responses from those we test the roles on. You can easily see the importance of clothing and appearance in this method of looking at the development of personality and self-concept.

As children we even practice for our eventual roles in life by dressing up as Daddy and Mommy in the games we play. Not only do we play Mommy and Daddy in these games, but we enact this role to become Mommy and Daddy. The clothing we wear in these games serves to make real the roles we play. So too does clothing serve to make real the roles we play in life.

Another view of the part clothing and appearance play in the development of personality and self-concept is called the looking glass effect. As we see our face, figure, and dress in the glass we are pleased (or otherwise) in what we see depending on how we imagine others see us. We look at ourselves not as we see ourselves but as we imagine others see us. If we feel others view us favorably, then our self-concept is enhanced. However, if we feel others view us unfavorably, then we experience negative feelings toward ourself.

Another approach holds that a person's self-concept is a social phenomenon. It develops as a result of the variety of roles taken on by the person in social reaction. The self reflects the responses of others toward the person as colored by the person's own skill in understanding how others see him. In other words, we build our self-concept by presenting a number of roles to others and evaluating their responses to either enhance or negate our opinion of ourselves. This evaluation is colored by how well we can imagine others see us. An interesting implication is that if we really knew how others saw us, we could in effect predetermine the response we receive from others and thus alter our concept of ourselves. We'll explore this later when we see how impression management through packaging our appearance can change even our personality by changing the response we receive from others.

So we can see how important clothing and appearance are at every stage of development. Since we develop all during our lives, then our clothing and appearance continue to be significant factors in the on-going development of our personalities and concept of ourselves. The final statement that "clothes make the man" becomes somewhat less trite and amusing in light of the above. We can recognize that our self-concept is determined by the responses of significant people in our life. Other people's pictures of us, however, will determine their reactions and responses to us, thus shaping how we think about ourselves. It is obvious, though, that the way we think we look to others is not always the way they see us, therefore we must understand the meanings or impressions that clothing and appearance convey to others and how others perceive clothing and appearance. Once we understand these meanings and their perceptions, the implications are staggering. Since we are shaped by the response of others to the roles we present, dominated by our clothing and appearance, if we package ourselves to elicit specific responses from others we can thus alter our own self-concept and personality.

For example, suppose for a moment that you had an important business meeting coming up that was essential to your future happiness and security. Let's say that you analyzed who was to be there and determined how they would interpret your clothing and appearance. Knowing that these people would respond favorably to the image of a successful, aggressive, honest, and knowledgeable salesman, you then presented this image by packaging your clothing and appearance in such a way that these individuals would accept you at face value as such a person. Having presented this role to them through impression management, you then received their favorable response of this image by their buying your product, services or ideas. Would not this response enhance your concept of yourself? Would you not also become more like this image you had presented? Psychologists tell us that we become what we think about most of the time. It should follow then that if we present an image of ourselves that is accepted at face value by others and is reinforced by their favorable response to this image, then we become more like this image we have presented, both in reality and in the way we see ourselves.

The fascinating thing about this impression management through your clothing and appearance is that the distinction between what we present to others and what we really are becomes blurred. We come to believe our own performances. Furthermore, the reactions and responses we receive from others make it all the more likely that we are what we pretend to be. When others accept the way we present ourselves and treat us as if we really are what we claim to be, do we not become what we present ourselves to be?

Obviously, dressing like a neurosurgeon will not make us a neurosurgeon. But if it is important for us to look successful and we package and present ourselves as successful, will not the predetermined responses we get make us successful? As we pointed out earlier, we can control the impression we make on people we meet in life by packaging ourselves through our dress and appearance to make them judge us favorably. The consequences of these favorable judgments are that people will respond to us favorably. In essence, we can control the image we present, and thus predict and control the reactions of those we meet and in doing so become the image we present. The main way we are judged is through our clothing and appearance. Therefore, by controlling our image not only are we what we wear but we become what we wear, to whose we meet in addition to ourselves. The young writer, Jonathan T. Schroder, has a motto on his desk — "Happiness is a man with a dream who is willing to pay for it." Success is a goal.

Want to change your life, then change your appearance. Want to be more successful, then package yourself to say what you want to those who are important to your success. The key, of course, is understanding what your clothing and appearance say to others and then packaging yourself accordingly. In the body of this book I will explain what your clothes say about you as well as how to package yourself to achieve specific goals. It is then up to you to decide whether or not it is important for you to do so.

To those who might say that using clothing to achieve certain goals smacks of manipulation or tampering with the minds of others, let me simply say this; to employ no thought or design in use of our resources, of which clothing and appearance are surely of great importance, is to expect that good things in life will happen through a series of happy accidents. Our clothing and appearance are tools we use to make our way through life.

7

WARDROBE DESIGN

In an interview on *The David Frost Show*, Robert Mitchum was asked the following question, "Bob, you've had some great roles in a lot of good films. How are you able to change the great character delineations from one film to another?" The camera cut to Robert Mitchum. Without a blink, he removed the cigarette from the corner of his mouth and said, "I think it was the wardrobe."

Although the clothing industry is a multi-billion dollar enterprise, the thrust of the industry is to design new clothes to sell to replace last year's new clothes. Little thought is given to what an individual's clothing says about him. Only one industry has ever made an in-depth study on the science of clothing. That's the motion picture industry. For seventy-five years that industry, through its wardrobe department, has researched, characterized and studied what the audience's reaction is to every article of clothing imaginable. They have used this knowledge to package actors to control the impressions conveyed to the audience, hence to control the audience's subconscious decisions about the character portrayed. Of course television uses the same wardrobe ideas. Wardrobe designers have developed the art of packaging an actor to control the audience reaction to the character portrayed into a science.

A good example of the depth and skill that wardrobe design has developed through the art or science of portraying character through packaging of appearance and clothing is illustrated by the approach taken by Leon Brauner as he designed the costumes for Kate in Shakespeare's *Taming of the Shrew*. Her volatile temper was symbolized and expressed throughout the play by repeated use of red. He explained that he started with a rich cherry velvet gown in the first scene, and as the action of the play progressed the tones of her succeeding costumes became more and more subdued:

> When the final curtain rises, we see Kate in a soft pink chiffon gown, the decolletage rounded and softened with pearl trim, her hair falls softly down her back. We feel reasonably sure that Petruchio, her husband, has finally tamed the shrew . . . Petruchio quizzes her about her constancy, we see her chin tip jauntily—then she turns quickly on her unsuspecting husband, and we see as she turns a brilliant red petticoat peek from beneath the pink chiffon making the final statement, as Shakespeare does, that one never really tames a shrew."★

★ Leon Brauner, "Character Portrayal Through Costume," speech presented at Western Regional Clothing and Textiles Meeting, Logan, Utah, October, 1964.

You will find a few classic actors and nostalgic Broadway buffs who claim that long before movies, they developed their own costumes. But make no mistake, it was a motion picture director who first observed, after leaving the set of a big western he was filming, that no one could tell the good guys from the bad guys. "Let's put white hats on the good guys and black hats on the bad guys." A science of what your clothes say about you was born. Like most inventions, it was born of need.

Hollywood quickly attracted the genius to use this new image technology. Genius was attracted in the beginning by the lure of money and the opportunity for creativity. It was the gold rush of Southern California. Hollywood paid in gold. But more important to the creative person, he was recognized and made famous. The only prerequisite to trying for this goal was the strong belief that he had greatness to contribute to the golden screen.

As silent movies matured, clothing became the visual short hand that instantly explained the scene. The rich had the biggest houses and their dress was always white. Their cars were the largest. Opulence blossomed everywhere. The poor people of the silver screen, not unlike their counterparts in real life, dressed in rags. Comedy evoked a recognition of class difference but it was only with the advent of the talkies that the motion picture industry began to realize the awesome power of the wardrobe department. They found that the actor's clothing told more about the actor than the actor's lines. In an amazingly short time the head of the wardrobe department had become, and still is, one of the studio's most influential people, frequently determining a character's success. Wardrobe designers categorized through research what items of clothing said throughout history in managing the impression given to the audience. Thus they could control the audience's reaction to this packaging. Many of the really big stars won't make a movie unless a certain wardrobe man does their clothing. Stars understand that their clothes establish their character—their lines just unfold the story.

Remember, first impressions are made on a subconscious level. You may not even be aware of what is being recorded. If a person is dressed wrong you may not know what is wrong—just that something is. Hollywood has made a science of it, but you recognize it too. You are already an expert at reading other people's clothes. You make your decisions about a person by what your eyes tell you about him, not what he says about himself. You have developed without intellectualizing this nonverbal skill in your own subconscious mind to a point beyond your own imagination. You instantly prepare yourself for any eventuality in a new relationship by measuring the person by what covers up 90 percent of him. We simplify it by calling it "first impression." But this doesn't happen overnight. Men start as little boys looking up to men who wore suits—dads and uncles, principals of schools, etc.— suits have always meant authority. Girls started playing with dolls and dressing them from childhood. But, as we have seen earlier, it is the media that trains the subconscious to compute clothing values on a person. That's where the Hollywood wardrobe department came in. They learned early how to compute clothes.

Let's take a familiar plot as an example. It is a lavish cocktail party. Titles are coming over the picture in the opening scene. As the titles clear, two fine-looking men walk into the scene together, both handsome and well-dressed. One cute girl turns to another and says, "That's Mr. Smith and Mr. Jones, both bankers and both available." If they stopped the picture right there and passed out cards which asked, "If you had $100,000 to deposit, which of these two men's banks would you deposit your money in?" 95 percent would answer, "Mr. Smith's bank."

Why? Because before the picture started shooting, the script was given to the head of the wardrobe department. He saw that at the end of the picture Mr. Jones was found to be the one who was stealing money from the bank and was the crook. But you saw it instantly. Somehow, Mr. Jones looked like a crook. The "somehow" was put there by the wardrobe department. The influence of the wardrobe department is evident in the opening of any film. Our hero is on a bus heading for a very important job interview in the city. He is dressed in a shiny polyester double-knit suit, brown-striped with three colors, striped color shirt, and the tie matches the light tan socks and shoes. We instantly know he is small-town, coming from a nice family of lower social and economic background. He's had a good middle-class education, probably at a small college. He gets off the bus and goes straight to a big building. We cut inside the building to a girl standing in conversation with her father. Right away we recognize Dad in his soft banker's gray flannel suit, white shirt, regimental tie, black shoes. Very successful. Dad is telling his daughter, "Girl, I am going to cut down your allowance for traveling. You're spending too much." She blows a kiss to him and says, "All right, but I love you anyway." She leaves. The hero gets off the elevator and bumps into the girl, almost knocking her down. He apologizes, saying he's on his way to a very important job interview with Mr. Big, who turns out, of course, to be her dad. Hero gets job. Girl gets hero.

Our girl is dressed as expected—the soft wool dress of classic design, matching shoes and purse of fine dark leather, scarf around her neck, and simple jewelry. The clothing told us that she was very wealthy, good eastern college, prep-school education, trustworthy, warm, desirable, but most of all, from that solid family background. As the film moves along, our girl and hero fall in love. Our heroes' wardrobe improves from "early nothing" to quality materials and conservative colors. Ties are regimental or solids and he is now projecting the same old family image as the old man himself. Just when all is going well for him, he meets an old ex-girl friend from college. Her clothes tell us that she comes from a rural town and lower economic background. Even though the other girl is married to a wealthy man, we sense she is a little more loose than she should be. She wears a bright red dress, plunging neckline, frills all over, and jewelry at every spot available. Her shoes and purse are expensive gold lame. Her makeup and hair style indicate where she has spent the day. Hero discovers that other girl is married to a wealthy man who he can see immediately is at least a millionaire. He's new money, from a lower social and economic background, modest education, semi-trustworthy. The heroine is upset by this encounter. A quarrel follows. However, hero and girl are reunited by an old family friend. We know he is quality because his clothes tell us of his upper class background and education. He is wealthy, old family, and trustworthy.

Now imagine this same film played in Red China. All the characters wear the same drab quilted coat and denim work pants throughout. It's easy to see that such a performance would have been at least flat, probably a disaster.

A movie's wardrobe can make or break a film. Likewise, your wardrobe can make or break you. The golden rule is to remember that the man who packages himself to turn off the least number of people gets the greatest opportunity.

In the remainder of this book you will find a step-by-step approach to packaging yourself as if you were a wardrobe designer. You will learn what your clothes say about you and how to plan your appearance to influence the actions of those you meet, the same as wardrobe designers elicit predetermined responses from the audience by packaging the actors. You will learn how to use your appearance as a tool to achieve specific goals, and in the process actually change your life by becoming the person you want to be.

"In a study of misdemeanor cases in Detroit's Recorder's Court it was found that defendants who appeared in court in work clothes had a much greater chance of going to jail than did defendants wearing suits or sport coats and ties."
—The Wall Street Journal

8

BUILDING A WARDROBE

Occupation, geography, climate, economy, versatility, and common sense are the determinants you should use when building a success-oriented wardrobe. The guiding principle for a man who understands that you are what you wear is: "Nothing wears as well as tradition. It reflects class repetition." Let's examine each of these factors to see how you can build a basic wardrobe.

Occupation

Your occupation is the most important influence on your wardrobe. Those of you whose occupations preclude wearing business attire must remember that you still are judged by what you wear in all factors of life. Be sure you follow the same guidelines as those who wear business attire in their occupations. There are two rules you must follow in building your basic wardrobe. First, your appearance must project that you are confident, reliable, and competent in your present position. Second, your dress should emulate those of your superiors so that you may be promoted within their circle without embarrassing them by your appearance. You're only promoted to a job you look like you belong in.

Although there are no hard and fast rules to be followed, here are two common-sense guidelines to be used as you let occupation influence your wardrobe.

First, analyze what your contemporaries are wearing. Obviously, bankers dress differently than sales executives. Study your industry or profession and identify your contemporaries as conservative (traditional), moderate, or flamboyant. Be sure your choice of styling and materials stays in the more conservative range exhibited by your contemporaries. Also, take pains to ensure that your clothes fit and are well-tailored. Sloppy fit and poor tailoring can draw almost as much adverse attention as funny or flamboyant clothes. By doing so, you will be representative of what you are, a successful member of your business or profession. To rise to the top and be respected in a group, you must first become a member of the group.

Second, observe what the men in your own company are wearing. Some companies are more formal or informal than others in the same field. You definitely don't want to look out of place in your own company. Pinpoint two or three successful men in your company who dress conservatively or traditionally and whose appearance gives them the right look of background and credibility. See what works for them. Study their accessories (ties, jewelry, attaché cases, etc.) but don't parrot them. Simply stay within a reasonable range of their wardrobe when choosing yours.

Climate and Geography

Climate and geography, although they don't necessarily go hand-in-hand, are the next two considerations in choosing your wardrobe. Climate will determine which materials and blends must be worn for your comfort. In colder climates you may choose more of the all-wool suits since they have a classic look and you can wear them almost year-round. In warmer climates, stick with the polyester, and wool blends even for the hot weather, also 100 percent wool light-weight suits. The 55 percent polyester and 45 percent wool blend is recommended because not only is it light weight but is the most durable in wear.

Always be sure that your suits have some wool in them since wool holds the shape of the suit and permits tailoring. In addi tion, wool is absorbent and breathes. Avoid double-knit at all costs. They pull, sag, and fade, along with shouting all the wrong things about you. If, in the deep South, you feel you must have a cotton or linen suit, then stick with the 100 percent cotton seersucker. However, you must be prepared to live with the wrinkled, crumpled look they have. You are better off with the cotton-polyester seersucker.

Geography is a factor, since widely separated parts of the country have different dress modes. Again, for these areas, such as Florida and California, stay within the more conservative boundaries exhibited by your contemporaries. When traveling to and through different geographical areas, never attempt to fool anyone that you are one of the locals by wearing those styles indigenous to those areas. Rely on the fail-safe outfits explained in Chapter Four since quality and tradition send out all the right signals about you anywhere. Remember, there are two kinds of fashion—true fashion and passing fashion. True fashion is line and classic balance while passing fashion is trimmings.

Economy

Economy is achieved by building your wardrobe with durability and versatility in mind. First, buy quality and not price. Clothing is an investment to be measured by how long it will last and how often you will wear it. Quality clothing will last longer than inexpensive goods, even though you will wear it more often since it looks and feels better. Therefore, you should stick with quality for durability rather than price. You should buy one good suit rather than two or three questionable suits for the same amount. Remember, today's suit was the seventy-five dollar suit of only a few years ago.

You achieve economy through versatility by initially choosing solid suits within the same color family so that your accessories (shirts, ties, belts, and shoes) are interchangeable. Another advantage of the solid suit over the stripe or the plaid is that by changing the shirt and tie, you change the outfit dramatically. Therefore, you can wear it more often in shorter periods of time. Furthermore, darker suits are more versatile since they may be worn more ways. The navy blue suit, for example, softened with a blue shirt and regimental tie, may be worn for business. The same suit with a white shirt and more formal tie can be worn to a dressy dinner or semi-formal affair. A word of caution here. Don't be misled into the mix and match trap. Never wear a suit coat as a sport coat. Never wear suit slacks with a blazer or sport coat. If the suit coat's cut and buttons are informal enough to pass as a sport coat, it's not a suit and you shouldn't own it. Likewise, the pants to your suits shouldn't be such a style or material that they could be worn informally. To make this mistake or have someone convince you it's possible, is to fool yourself, but no one else. Suits are traditionally recognized for situations of a serious nature. Sport coats are for less serious occasions. The blazer suit, a hybrid of the two, is neither fish nor fowl. Consequently, it is seldom appropriate for either situation and incongruous in most. The blazer suit has almost as many negative connotations as the leisure suit. The blazer suit is a blatant attempt to sacrifice good taste and tradition for economy.

Visual Shorthand

Since people judge you by what you wear, you can start building a basic wardrobe by utilizing what I call "visual shorthand" when you evaluate your present wardrobe. First, imagine a color chart of ten: Making number ten the dominant figure suit, which is black, then navy blue, charcoal gray, navy blue pin stripe, etc. down to one—all white—the Kentucky Colonel. You must always stay five or above for business or to be taken seriously. Next, using the color chart and the previous criteria (occupation, geography, climate) go through your wardrobe to see what you can or cannot wear according to those determinants. You will realize that you have been wearing some of your suits inappropriately; i.e., a number three color suit for business. Others you will realize you can't wear at all—too flamboyant, double-knit, or unsuitable for your occupation. Now we're ready to rebuild the basic minimum wardrobe.

Basic Minimum Wardrobe

Suits—three vested or non-vested (personal preference)

business suits (number five or above). These should be solid suits in the same color family and tone. One solid navy blue pinstripe 55 percent polyester and 45 percent wool vested suit. This suit may be worn for business or formal wear. One navy blue and one solid medium gray (dark) 55 percent polyester and 45 percent wool vested suit.

One navy blue natural shoulder blazer with gold buttons— 55 percent polyester and 45 percent wool. This may be worn year-round and is appropriate for some business occasions as well as all informal occasions.

Two pairs of trousers—one solid gray (medium to dark) year-round blend; one gray patterned or solid tan.

Twelve long sleeve dress shirts—six white; two blue; two ecru; one stripe; and one tattersall (casual).

Two pairs of black shoes, to be rotated daily—one wing tip lace; and one dress slip-on.

One black belt with plain gold or brass buckle (1-1/2" - 1 3/4").

One classic beige raglan shoulder raincoat.

One dozen black, over the calf socks.

Since your basic suits and blazer are in the same color family and tone, all your shirts and ties will be interchangeable. By rotating these shirts and ties, wearing and not wearing the vests, and using the blazer for casual wear, you achieve a large number of different outfits. Remember, since your suits are solids, each time you change the shirt and tie you give the suit a completely different look. Wearing the vest or not wearing it gives each suit additional versatility.

Adding to the Basic Minimum Wardrobe

When adding to your basic minimum wardrobe, remember that solid suits are more versatile. Don't get into stripes or plaids until you have at least three solid suits. When you do start adding stripes and plaids, stay conservative with a narrower stripe or the mooted understated patterns, such as shadow plaids. By taking proper care of your suits, rotating your wardrobe, and following the advice in this book, you will find that your clothes don't wear out, but rather you get tired of them and replace them.

Further Economy

Remembering that your wardrobe is not a luxury but rather an investment that will pay off for you—buy quality. Look for sales on merchandise you've seen in your store. Buy for spring in the fall and fall in the spring.

9

MATERIALS

The materials you use in building your wardrobe are very important to the image you want to project. Certain materials, such as cashmere, have a high status connotation. Others, such as double-knit polyester, have a very low status representation. The important thing to remember is that you must analyze the situations you will be in and determine which materials say the right thing for those particular situations. As a guiding principle, plan your appearance not to offend or be least likely to offend. Don't attempt to overwhelm or overpower those you meet by the opulence of your clothing. Simply try to package yourself so that you do not distract or offend.

Wool

Wool and wool-polyester blends in the classic, traditional patterns and weaves are the only material I recommend in building a wardrobe that says the correct things about you. Wool is a natural material which breathes easily, absorbs moisture, and holds its shape very well. Wool, with its irregularities in weave and varied texture, has a deep, rich, natural look that suggests character. The wool-polyester blend retains the advantages of wool, along with being lighter weight and more wrinkle resistant. Before we concentrate on wool and wool blends, let's first look at some of the other materials available and their drawbacks.

Cotton, Linen, Silk and Blends

The principal shortcoming of suits made from cotton and linen is that they have a crumpled, wrinkled look that is difficult to take seriously. In addition, they rarely come in colors suitable for anything but the most informal occasions. Even when blended with polyester, the cotton or linen suit will bag and lose its shape. Many character actors have almost built their careers around the negative connotations suggested by the wrinkled, dirty, cotton or linen suit. Silk suits lack durability and wear poorly. More importantly, they project an ostentatious, overstated look, which is offensive to many people. In addition, the silk has become the symbol of the shifty, nouveau riche character—quite possibly the gangster. These negative connotations of the silk suit are not for you.

Polyesters

There have been advancements in the development of synthetic materials. Unfortunately, the suit made from these materials is not acceptable in any successful wardrobe. Granted, the all-polyester suit is claimed to be wrinkle proof, machine washable, and travel tested. However, it is uncomfortably hot in the summer, cold in the winter, and lacks the rich feel and pleasing textures of wool or wool blends. In addition, the polyester suit is unmistakably shiny, suffers from snags and pulls, is easily burned, and loses its shape quite easily. And if all that isn't enough, the polyester suit is instantly recognized as inexpensive and artificial. Consequently, the polyester suit, no matter what the color, weave, or price range, projects an impoverished background, modest education, and "new boy in town" look. These negative connotations have an immediate effect on the people you meet.

Wool and Wool Polyesters

Wools may be divided into worsted and woolens. Worsteds are tightly woven wool materials which are wrinkle and dirt resistant. Woolens are heavier, more loosely woven materials. Both have the rich natural look and feel which reflects character and background. Worsteds such as sharkskin, serge, covert, and gabardine drape and tailor well. Woolens, such as tweed, shetland, and flannel are softer, comfortable, and more casual. The blending of wool with polyester produces a materials which maintains the quality look and resistant advantages of the polyester. The wool-polyester blend is a lighter weight material which can be used for wrinkle free summer clothes. The 55 percent polyester and 45 percent wool is the recommended blend for year-round wear. This blend is very durable, wears well, and is wrinkle- resistant.

Hand

The feel of a material is referred to as the "hand" of the material. Quite often the fabric in less expensive suits will look almost the same as the material in a more expensive quality suit. A manufacturer of inferior clothing will imitate a popular expensive fabric with materials of poorer quality. In the trade, this is known as a "knock-off." You can tell the difference in the "hand" or feel of the two fabrics. A good fabric will feel smooth and supple, not harsh. If squeezed and brushed, it will spring back into shape without wrinkles. In addition to the quality of the fabric the unseen workmanship, the canvas in the coat front, the collar construction, the pocket and coat lining, even the thread and buttons are factors which influence the life and appearance of a well-made garment. Since the life expectancy, given good care, of a quality garment is several times that of an inferior make, it is more economical to buy quality.

Label

The material content of each garment is required by law to be listed by the manufacturer on a label attached to the garment. On suits and sport coats this label will be found on the left sleeve near the cuff. On slacks, the label will be found near the waistband. Always check the label to find the material content when shopping. Virgin wool will be listed as such or simply wool. Reprocessed and reused wool are listed as such. Virgin wool has superior wearing strength over reprocessed or reused wool. Wool and wool-polyester blends will be listed as percentages. As I mentioned, the 55 percent polyester and 45 percent wool blend is the best. The least acceptable blend would be the 70 percent polyester and 30 percent wool.

Weight

The weight of the fabric is a little understood but very important consideration when you build your wardrobe. Weight of the fabric is determined by the number of ounces of yarn woven in each square yard of material. Since the modern suit is designed for appearance and image, not warmth, the eight to ten ounce weight of fabric is the most practical since it can be worn year-round. The winter suit should not exceed twelve ounces. Sport coats may be of fourteen or fifteen ounces, but should not exceed this figure. Once you understand that the weight of the fabric, along with the material content, determines the warmth of the fabric, you can see why a 100 percent light weight wool tropical worsted can be cooler in the summer heat than a 100 percent polyester.

Types of Fabric

Now that you understand weight, materials, and feel of fabrics, you are ready to consider the classic, traditional fabrics woven of wool, or a wool-polyester blend, which say all the right things about you. Deviations from these recommended fabrics are at your own risk. Remember, even the man who doesn't own one, always recognizes a quality car when it goes by.

10

A GREAT MEN'S STORE

The first step in the art of packaging yourself through planning your appearance is to locate a store where you can confidently find and economically purchase your wardrobe.

You must find a great men's store.

But it is important to understand what a great men's store really is. It is not a government subsidized agency designed to cover up men appearing in public. Instead, it's a profit making enterprise (hopefully) in which someone has invested great sums of money because he enjoys clothes and people. The important point, however, is to find the store that is right for you.

It's fair to say that there doesn't exist a clothier who doesn't sincerely feel he is helping his customers. Unfortunately, there are many varied backgrounds, values, and lifestyles which must be catered to. Since each store owner sees his store fulfilling a different need, you must determine what your goals are and find the store which supplies the necessary wardrobe for your personal packaging. Although most of my remarks will be addressed to the man who desires to package himself for success in the business world, the mechanics of finding the right store for yourself hold true no matter what your goals are.

The first criterion to use in finding the right store for you is to study the clothing and appearance of the store owner or manager and his employees. The owner or manager of the store for you must present an appearance similar to the one you wish for yourself. Does his appearance project the taste and credibility that you want to project? Do his employees exemplify or contradict his taste and credibility? As in most important areas of life, consistency is important, so does all his merchandise reflect a consistent approach to dress habits for gentlemen? Is the quality of the merchandise consistent or haphazard?

The store for the man who wishes to change his life for the better by packaging his appearance for success will be owned or managed by an individual whose appearance suggests an upper socio-economic background, which is the same look you're striving for. Frankly, you cannot sell quality unless you look quality. In addition, the right store for you will be easy to find because the owner or manager will express his concern for his customers by hand picking everything in the store. This will be readily apparent in the consistent quality of the clothing from overcoats down to socks. If such consistency is not easily discerned, then such a store is no place for you to use for your packaging. The professional clothing store operator who hand-picks his merchandise with a particular type of customer in mind, defines his market in the process. He buys specifically for a certain type of customer, and consequently develops a following in that market. His own education, taste, interests, and background give him the ability to cater to that type of market. For those who wish for success in business, you must find a men's store run by a successful businessman who caters to other successful businessmen. This store will provide the wardrobe you need to package yourself as a successful businessman.

As a professional, the right clothing store operator will be able to guide you in planning and structuring your appearance. The wise man does not make decisions about his life without consulting a professional in the field. Your health rates a family doctor. Your future and your family's security requires an insurance expert. Your broker handles your investments. Does it not then follow that since your appearance is so important to your success in life, you select and confide in a professional when you make decisions on wardrobe? Remember—the professional you choose must project the image that you plan for yourself. If he doesn't he certainly cannot help you.

Once you have found this professional and his store, start going in often and getting to know him and his salesmen. Drop by if only to say hello. Find out what colors and fabrics are expected in. Decide if these fit your overall plans. Explain to him your plans for packaging your appearance. Familiarize him with your business, your goals, and your needs. By becoming a known entity to him, he can help evaluate your future, give you direction, and prevent you from making snap judgment purchases.

You have now climbed over the great wall. You are going to your lawyer, your CPA, your doctor and now you can confide in your wardrobe advisor (about your image). You should develop a relationship with your clothier so that he doesn't feel he has to sell you something. Instead, he works with you to help you plan the appropriate image you want to present.

Unfortunately, this working relationship can seldom be

found in a department store. The truly outstanding men's wear businesses were built on a one-to-one relationship, since each good men's store sells one distinctive "look." This look cannot be something for everyone, and that is why department stores are relatively unsuccessful in developing that one-to-one relationship in their men's departments. Neiman-Marcus, Marshall Fields, and a few others do it well but, generally speaking, few department stores are capable of developing this relationship. Their salespeople are not trained on individual needs of fit, image, and tailoring, but rather their training is oriented toward mass market appeal and selling whatever is available in their merchandise at any particular time. However, let's not blame the department stores' salespeople. They do what they are told to do. There is seldom any communications between sales personnel and buyers for department stores. The buyer selects clothing for the stores using criteria on what will appeal to the mass market. He buys what is faddy or "in" and can be sold to casual shoppers who really are not planning a general approach to their image control through appearance. In addition, the high turnover of personnel puts the customer in an insecure position when he continually finds new faces to wait on him.

Once you have found a store which you can call your own, watch for sales. Since you frequently drop in to look over the merchandise, you should be familiar with the quality and price of the merchandise. Therefore, you will be able to determine what really is on sale and is a bargain. By watching for sales, which are normally seasonal, you stand a good chance of saving money on a real value. In addition, by sticking with your store you will eliminate the chances of shopping other stores during their sales. You are familiar with the merchandise, know the owner, operator, and employees, and can feel secure in buying sale merchandise. In addition, your relationship with your store should be a life-long one, provided conditions remain the same. This relationship should continue to develop and mature through out your life since your clothing and appearance is a matter of life-long importance.

Remember, find a store whose operator and employees exemplify the image and look which you want to present to the world. Develop a relationship which is mutually rewarding to both you and the store. The store must be consistent in quality and the merchandise hand picked by the operator. Become known to the operator and his employees so that they can guide you in your packaging approach by knowing what your goals and needs are. Finally, be familiar with the merchandise and prices, so that you can shop with a confidence during sales times for the best economical structuring of appearance.

Unfortunately, most men in this country approach the purchase of their clothing with little planning and less foresight. They put a false grasp of economics before purpose in buying their wardrobes. For this reason, the American male has sometimes been referred to as the "Great American Junk Buyer." You must be aware of a few facts and be armed with a thought-out plan when you shop to build your packaging wardrobe. Let's take a realistic look at the act of shopping.

First a bargain is not a bargain if it's being sold for half-price because it's usually leader-item merchandise. Or, simply put, junk. It's there to draw the price buyer into the store. If you buy here, you are throwing your money away. Once you realize what you have done, you will not wear it anyway, or you will spend most of your time apologizing for the way you look when you do wear it. In addition, many big stores have chosen certain times to move all their mistakes. They send all South Mall's junk on to the North Mall, and the

North Mall's junk to the West Mall, etc. And here *he* comes, The Great American Junk Buyer!

Without advice he tends to buy bargains. Price becomes his primary consideration. He'll buy whatever is on sale—regardless. "Sale" is the golden word he can trust because it says 30 percent or 50 percent off! That's probably why most of our clothes closets are poorly lit, to hide our mistakes. Once he has spotted a sale, he's hooked. He goes in and there are three suits in his size. So, he buys all three. He isn't worried about fit because they are all 40 regular and he says "I'm a 40 regular." He wants his wife to buy his shirts and ties whenever and wherever she sees another big sale because that stuff doesn't matter. And of course he just picks up his underwear at any bargain counter or basement sale. Who cares? No one sees them anyway. He usually buys shoes himself because they have to fit, but he buys only during sales because all he does is walk in them. When he gets this junk, he gets a real kick out of his mix and match efforts. It proves once more that he is a great bargain hunter. It also makes him look like he borrowed his clothes from four different people. Nothing really goes together and a year later the belted-back suit is out of style (assuming it was ever in). He keeps on wearing it because it still fits — well, sort of. The other suit his buddy picked. It gets a lot of laughs, so he wears that one too. The third suit, the iridescent green, he only wore three times, because it faded. No one ever sees it any more. The ties and shirts his wife buys are beautiful purple and chartreuse, but this year they do not go with blue and green suits. Underwear, well it just comes and goes in the washing machine anyway. No one sees it, except of course, the guys at the golf course and tennis club, but they are men, too, so who cares? People cannot judge you by funny underwear, right? Wrong! The members of your country club are probably some of the most influential people you will come across and they do not wear funny underwear. They will put you in the "funny" category if you do.

There are, of course, real bargains, but they are difficult to recognize because the real cost of clothing is not necessarily the price on the tag. To discover the real cost you must take the price you paid for it, divide by the number of times you have worn it, and give yourself leeway for pleasure, self-confidence, and image value. It may sound a bit complicated at first, but in business it's called amortization. Remember the sale suit that was marked down, not the suit you wanted, but the price was right. You said, "Gee, I've got to take it," so you grabbed it. Only to find out you would wear it just four times before realizing what a terrible suit it was and that is why they dumped it on you. Now, that was an expensive suit. While the other one you rationalized paying the regular going rate for, you are still wearing, still getting compliments on and, most importantly, still generating an image that says all the right things about you. That suit is a real bargain.

How much is too much? Is it better to pay always a marked down price for a suit and wear it for a year, then throw it away? The Salvation Army will not take it as a tax write-off. No junk accepted. Or should you pay the going rate for a garment that gives you an emotional lift each time you wear it; that gives you a calculated response of credibility, and commands the respect of everyone you meet. This is the suit that gives you security—not the cheap one. Don't be the Great American Junk Buyer. The cheap clothing you and I have bought in our lifetime has one thing in common—it was bought with the thought of practicality and not emotional impact. One way or another we are still paying for that.

As you can see, the Great American Junk Buyer loses money rather than saves it. He has no permanent relationship with a store he can trust. He has no plan to coordinate and plan his wardrobe needs. His mix-and-match clothing that he has bought at various sales only makes him look ridiculous.

You can avoid the pitfalls of the junk buyer by employing a little analysis and planning of your wardrobe needs. First, balance your wardrobe by analyzing your activities and then determining your wardrobe needs by weighing these activities. For example, if when you analyze your activities, you find that 80 percent of your time is consumed by your work, then 80 percent of your wardrobe should be work-oriented clothing. Conversely, if you are fortunate enough to spread the majority of your time in leisure activities, then weight your wardrobe accordingly. This sounds simple and perhaps too basic, yet very few people actually follow through on this concept. Take a complete and honest inventory of your clothing, separating each item by function. Next, make a realistic appraisal to see if your clothes match your activities on a percentage basis. Then draw up a list of clothing needs necessary to balance your wardrobe. Stick to it. Carry it with you when you shop. This way you can avoid the impulse of buying of the great looking sport coat on sale which in all practicality you will wear two or three times a year. Approach your wardrobe with planning and care. Be firm! Know what you want, and wait for the sale at your men's store to get it. Do not be trapped into buying sale merchandise you neither need nor will wear.

After you have made a firm and honest appraisal of your wardrobe needs by activity, use the inventory you developed as a working guide to planning the image you want to present. Later, after finishing the sections in this book detailing what your clothes actually say about you and how to use them to package your appearance, use this inventory as a living control of wardrobe, selecting by adding or replacing items of clothing with a specific purpose in mind for each. This way you will save a considerable amount of money simply by organizing your wardrobe on a functional plan, thus eliminating unwanted or unneeded clothing.

In short, be sophisticated enough to know what "sales" really are. Coordinate your accessories by buying specifically for the suit or sport coat outfit you have in mind. Do not buy accessories independently, and then try to make them work later. Realize that quality, even if more expensive, is more economical since you will wear quality much longer and more frequently, not to mention the aesthetic value you receive from wearing fine clothing. Analyze and weight your clothing needs according to your lifestyle, so that you can realistically plan your wardrobe to meet your needs. Keep a running activity weight inventory of your wardrobe to help you plan and package your appearance to achieve your goals.

11

HOW TO BUY A SUIT

The suit is the most important single item in packaging yourself. It is the canvas on which you paint your personality, background, and future for the world to see. The material, cut, and tailoring of your suit will convey meanings to those you meet. By sticking with the classic materials outlined in Chapter 9, you will avoid making mistakes in your impression through choosing inappropriate materials. However, the fit and cut of your suit also send unmistakable signals to those you come in contact with. Tight, closely cut clothing presents an image which is hard to justify in business, yet great for pleasing women. Again, you must analyze what it is you want to say with your appearance, and choose accordingly.

For business there is only one suit, the traditional, classic business suit. The leisure suit, the blazer suit, some of the designer suits, the jump suit, or even the "zoot" suit, you name it, all are inappropriate for success in the business world.

American business is run by a group of men who look like they belong where they are. They adopt similarities so they can identify themselves to each other. If you would be considered as one, you had better adopt the suit they wear—the classic traditionally styled business suit.

Before you accuse me of saying that American businessmen are mindless in their choice of clothing and have an unwillingness to change or progress because they stay with the same basic uniform — the business suit, let me repeat what I just said: They adopt similarities to they can identify each other. As a recurring theme in this book, the point is made that you are judged by your clothing and appearance. Businessmen, consciously or instinctively, adopt the business suit as protective clothing in the jungle of business. They dress so that they may identify each other as at least citizens if not higher status individuals in the business world. If it is your desire to not be identified as a serious member of the business world, then simply wear anything but the classic, traditional suit.

The blazer suit, a combination idea, has been promoted as an economy measure. However, the negative feelings generated by this composite, neither fish nor fowl, made it inappropriate for even the most casual business occasion. If your business is casual enough for a blazer or sports jacket, then wear one, not this combination.

The designer suit is just what the name implies. It is designed to conform to someone's idea of what would be good for the gentleman this season.

Designer names have become the new brand names of the men's stores. When a man is choosing between two similar suits or sport coats, a designer label may be just the added incentive to make him buy.

But we must be aware of each designer's position in the market in order to choose one whose clothes will suit us.

Think of all the great designers as similar to the Big Four automakers: Each has proven his ability in design and production, and our job is to find out which one is right for each of us at this point in our lives and careers. And, of course, we must find a designer at prices that fit our wallets.

Of course, no one designer is perfect for everyone. Each man is built differently, and there is no perfect build. Try to find a designer line or label that fits your body and makes you look good. Once you find a label that works for you, stick with it.

The incongruities represented by buying high fashion, designer clothes for business can be easily understood if one thinks about a gentleman usually described as a high status businessman or professional. Most people would use the term "English" or "British." In fact, the man is probably a well-to-do English businessman.

However, the most interesting fact is that in France, the world capital for high fashion, this gentleman's attire represents to the French the style of the true gentleman. The fitted suit with vest, bowler hat, black, polished shoes, and a rolled umbrella with wooden handle, epitomizes the style of the true gentleman. Even though this London style is rarely worn by Frenchmen, it unmistakably represents cultural distinctiveness that is recognized in the heart of the fashion world.

The conclusion to be drawn from this is that while designer suits do say something about you, do they say what you want them to say to your business associates. The high fashion designer suit is fine if you want to captivate women, but if you want to captain industry, stick with the classic, traditional business suit, which is recognized and accepted anywhere in the world.

In addition to the styling of the suit, the stitching, buttons, lapels, eyelets, cuffs, in short, *everything* must be classic and traditional. Don't worry about dressing up your image with fancy stitching or special lapels. The dressing up of your image can be accomplished with your shirt, tie, and other accessories. Let the suit play its rightful role in your image—the basic, correct background upon which to structure your appearance. As such, the suit is an extremely versatile canvas. For example, it may be used as a weapon. Simply wear dark, authoritative colors for intimidation. It may be used as a relaxant or a means of putting people at ease by wearing the more friendly color, either medium gray or tan. Whatever you use your business suit for, remember, the impression you create is shaped by what covers 90 percent of your body—your clothes. In addition, the suit composes 80 percent of your visual clothing. Therefore, the proper classic, business suit is the basic protective coloring to be used to package yourself in the business world.

But first, you must know how to buy it.

Preparation

After you have located *your* men's store, checked with several friends who deal there regularly to find out the do's and don't (i.e., which tailor to ask for, special salesman, etc.) you are ready to go in and meet the owner and manager. This first meeting is very important. It will set the physical stage and emotional tone for your future relationship. Wear your best outfit. This will establish three things to the owner or manager and his staff: (1) you're serious; (2) you want the best; and (3) you expect service. Walk in wearing a tee-shirt and tennis shoes and no one will give you a second glance. Explain your wardrobe needs and goals. Don't be extravagant, simply be sincere. You don't have to give the impression you're going to buy out the store, but you should be serious and cordial. In short, make them want your business.

Next, look over your wardrobe and decide the type of suit you need and what you'll use it for. Consider the factors explained in Chapter 8, "Building A Wardrobe." Use the visual shorthand you now understand to decide what you want this suit to say about you. Buy with purpose—not emotion.

Materials

Study the chapter on materials. Decide which material you want based on climate and your occupation. Remember, most men today don't buy suits for warmth, since they spend little time out-of-doors. Consequently, the best material for you budget- wise is the 100 percent tropical wool or polyester-wool blend for year-round use. As your wardrobe builds and your budget permits, you can look at all wools, such as a beautiful gray or dark blue flannel, for six to nine months a year wear. Harris Tweeds and other heavier materials for sport coats are usually a luxury until your budget allows you to choose seasonal outfits.

Size and How to Find It

Most clothing salesmen allow the customer to tell them the size they wear. The salesman then spends his time trying to somehow make the customer fit that size. Practically all customers wear the wrong size most of their lives—through vanity. They're convinced that their physical proportions haven't changed since their early twenties. Once a 42 regular, always a 42 regular, forgetting that after thirty the body starts to shift and change proportions. Consequently, no matter what the salesman knows, or what he says about fit and service, he allows the customer to buy a suit that doesn't fit, but pleases the customer's vanity.

Suit size is based on chest measurement. The length of the garment is based on height (see Chapter 12, "Line and Balance). However, these standards vary from manufacturer to manufacturer. In addition, these measurements are affected by the cut and styling of the suit. Therefore, the only way to see if the suit fits is to try on the jacket, not look at the label. Don't hesitate to try on jackets one or two sizes in either direction from what you think your suit size is. Try different lengths (i.e., regular and long) of the same size. These two considerations are doubly important should your store stock from several different manufacturers or have a variety of styles available. If you try the suit on and it fits and looks right, then that's your size. Remember, when you wear the suit, no one is ever going to ask you what size it is. You either look great or you don't.

The Shoulder

The most important part of the fit is the shoulder. That is where the real money in labor and workmanship of the suit is concentrated. Half of the people I talk to try on a suit only to say, "The waist is too big." When I reply, "What about the shoulders?" they give me a quizzical look as if to say: "Are they supposed to fit too?" The shoulder must fit for the suit to be comfortable. The waist, the sleeves, the pants and the shape of the suit can be altered once you find a fit in the shoulders. If you choose a suit that looks great but doesn't fit in the shoulder, you'll soon stop wearing it. Be man enough to blame yourself for choosing the wrong size, don't blame the suit. Remember, find a good comfortable fit in the shoulders. Have the rest of the suit altered by a good tailor. You will look great and feel great. This is the key to enjoying a good fit throughout your life.

The Suit is an Investment

You should now look at your clothing as an investment. Consequently, you should buy the blue-chips, the classic or traditional quality suit. This is the clothing investment that pays off in the long run. It wears longer, never goes out of style and never changes. Equally important, you will get an emotional lift every time you put it on. If you know you are wearing the correct clothes, you have freed yourself from one of the major concerns of life. One of my friends, a lawyer, came into my store one day and said, "Guess what I paid for this suit? It's a famous make." He then went on to explain that someone had contacted his firm, told my customer and his associates that he's gotten a good buy on some famous maker suits and was selling them for ninety-nine dollars each. My friend concluded by saying that he had bought three of them. I felt sorry for him as I looked at the suit and wanted to say, "Didn't it ever occur to you that if these suits were any good, any retailer in town would be happy to buy the entire lot from him at that price? He wouldn't have to hustle them around town." Instead, like anyone else who has just watched the barrel go over the waterfall, I just said, "Wonderful" and dropped it. Think about it the next time a deal is offered you. If you stop and realize that men's suits are marketed like any other retail item, it's not hard to see what quality material and labor goes into a quality suit. The manufacturer has to make a profit, the retailer has to make his mark-up, and there must be some money for alterations if they are included in the price. Therefore, you must expect to pay a minimum retail price at a quality men's store for a suit of reasonable quality tailored in a classic material. To be safe, you must expect to pay a retail price at your store you have learned to trust for a truly quality suit.

Remember, you can save a considerable amount of the retail price by watching for sales at *your* men's store and buying off season. Again, I can't stress enough that the quality suit is less expensive in reality because you wear it more often and it lasts longer. The vested suit gives you two different looks. However, if you prefer non-vested suits, you can expect to reduce the retail price by twenty-five to fifty dollars.

What to Look For

First, stay with the classic materials (see Chapter 9). A poor fabric will not wear well and each time the suit is dry- cleaned it will have a noticeable effect on the material. The poorer material loses shape and develops a tired, bedraggled look. Second, check the lapel edges and other seams to make sure there is no puckering or bubbling. Make sure the collar lies flat against your neck. If it doesn't, the collar must be shortened. Check between your shoulder blades for wrinkling. Again, these wrinkles can be altered, but seldom will be unless you request it. Next, check the lining to see how well it has been set into the jacket. Make sure the lining does not sag below the edge of the jacket, yet does have an expansion pleat. Check the sleeves to see that the lining doesn't extend past the cuff. See that ,the suit has real horn or bone buttons and that the buttonholes are not ragged.

The Second Fitting

The second fitting is definitely not secondary in importance. The second fitting is the crucial test in the purchase of your suit. Always give yourself plenty of time to try on the suit. Make sure the tailor is present should any additional alterations be needed. Obviously, the tailor will be reluctant to make any further changes. Don't be afraid to insist on them if needed, since you are the final authority. You're paying for it. Study the suit in a full-length mirror. Here are some key observations you must make.

1. Collar and Shoulders—Collar should be snug on the neck and there should be no ripples or straining between shoulder blades.
2. Sleeves—The sleeves of the jacket should end at the middle of your wrist bone, with the shirt sleeve extending one-fourth inch to one-half inch beyond. Since almost everyone has one arm longer than the other, make sure the tailor checks the length of both sleeves.
3. Jacket—There are two potential problem areas. One shoulder may be lower than the other. Your chest and shoulder may be larger and stronger on one side. Make sure the tailor has allowed for these conditions if they exist. The length of the jacket should be even in front; if not, one shoulder may have to be built up or the jacket buttons adjusted.
4. Vents—Whether single or double vent, the jacket should hang straight and there must be enough overlap in the vents to prevent them from opening out when you move.
5. Pants—After alterations in the waist and seat, the pants should fall straight, with the crease centered ahead. If crease is not centered, the pants must be altered by shifting the inside seams. Do not allow the crease to be changed by simply pressing a new crease. If the seams

are not shifted, the crease will be back off-center when they are pressed after the first dry cleaning. Insist on an alteration here, not a simple pressing-in of a new crease. They should be neither too tight nor bag in the seat or crotch. Try sitting down to see if they are comfortable.

6. Length—The pant cuff length measurement should not be taken until the second fitting. If there are any major alterations in the waist, seat, and crotch, the length of the pants will be affected. Again, since many people have one leg shorter than the other, make sure the tailor measures both legs. The plain bottom pant should just touch the top of the shoe without breaking. The pant leg should slant about one-half inch toward the top of the heel. This give a look of a longer pant leg when walking away. The cuffed pant leg should again just touch the top of the shoe without breaking.

You know more about buying a suit than 95 percent of your fellow Americans. Good luck, and stick to your guns. You get what you pay for and ask for. One last word of caution is appropriate. Beware of the signs reading "Special Purchase." This is usually the kiss of death fronting for shoddy material, poor workmanship, or outdated, unsaleable goods. This sign usually leads to a journey into the unknown.

You now understand how to buy a suit. In addition, you realize the suit is the basic ingredient in the packaging concept that you have decided for yourself. By staying with the classic, traditional style business suit you immediately establish your self as a contemporary of your business associates. The fit can make or break your appearance, so don't be afraid to insist on what is right for you.

What's Suitable Picking a Summer Wardrobe

The changing of the seasons gives us a vital feeling of renewal. Even people living in areas of the country that experience no drastic seasonal change still have seasonal clothing changes, if only in the evening. The important thing here is not to loose the look you have worked so hard to achieve. Summer for the businessman is not an escape hatch to go to the office in baggy, unpressed slacks, short sleeved or white shoes. As sure as rent, food bills, and car payments keep coming all summer, business pressures know no season.

The basic difference in what we call a summer suit is in the weight of the material. There are many summer suits that are appropriate and I'll cover as many as I can here. Armed with the right information, you can get an idea of which one would be best for you.

First, the "executive" suits. Remember our color scale of 1 to 10, starting with the white Kentucky colonel suit as No. 1, and graduating in darkness on up to No. 10 — the midnight blue, charcoal gray, and black. Even during the summer, for important business meetings or any place where a personal judgment on someone else's part may affect your future, you should wear 8, 9, or 10, depending on the occasion or the seriousness of the situation.

These suits come in: 100 percent wool, 55 percent polyester/45 percent wool, 50 percent wool/50 percent silk, 50 percent silk/30 percent wool/20 percent polyester and 25 percent wool/25 percent linen/50 percent silk. Always check the little white ticket on the sleeve of each suit. (The U.S. government requires that all manufacturers put the material content on each suit. Your suit must fit into or hit near these percentages. Note that wool was in every summer tropical suit listed here.) These are the fail-safe fabrics. You will enjoy the price tags, as summer tropicals are usually less expensive than the fall wools and flannels. These suits are a good buy because they can be worn year-round in most states. Men no longer look to the suit to keep them warm. They have heated automobiles, offices, and homes to take care of that.

The next grouping is just plain summer suits. These are the traditional "hey-it's-summertime-again" suits. If purchased correctly these classic summer suits become great investments, as they never change or go out of style. The classic seersucker comes in three good colors: white-blue, white-brown and white- grey or black. They come two ways — 100 percent cotton or 65 percent polyester/35 percent cotton. The all-cotton is tough when it comes to cleaning and pressing. The poly/cotton blend is more functional and it resists dirt and holds a pressing best.

You and you alone must make the decision as to what selection you will make. But keep in mind the finer the stripes the more conservative you are perceived. The wider stripes are considered more flamboyant.

Make sure your summer suit has the same lapel, soft shoulder, and cut as the classic traditional suit.

"Some years ago Loudon Wainwright gave us an interesting look at how the tailor of his first London tailored suit covered up what Wainwright referred to as a substantial secret. "Before leaving Perry's shop, I asked Mr. Perry, the tailor, if there had been any special problems in making the suit. Evasive at first, the tailor finally admitted: "Well, sir, . . . you have a rather long body and that's a thing we have to minimize. We had to lengthen your legs, so to speak, and shorten your body. Nothing serious, really, and it worked out quite well." This was the first time I'd heard of this particular defect in my structure, and I took another look in the mirror. Mr. Perry was right. It was impossible to tell now, where my short legs ended and my long body began."

—Loudon Wainwright "Disguising the Man," *Life*

12

LINE AND BALANCE

The principles of line, balance, and harmony when related to the cut and pattern you choose in your clothing are very important to the image you want to present. First, you must remember that no one has a perfect physical shape. The person who looks perfect has learned how to apply, line, balance, and harmony to his clothing, so that his physical problems are camouflaged. For example, two men of the same height, weight, and measurements may be completely different physical types. Obviously, they must have their clothes tailored quite differently to project visual balance and proportionate images. The first principle you must understand is the impact visual illusion has on your silhouette.

Visual Perception—The importance of the silhouette of your clothing can hardly be overstated. Your silhouette is the overall visual picture you present which is received by the mind's eye of those you meet. Fortunately, this visual picture is not simply picked up in the mind's eye like a camera image and presented to the brain. Instead, studies indicate that we do not always see things as they exist, but rather that seeing is combined with judgment. The brain seeks to establish some order or meaning and, hence, interprets what the eyes see.

Understanding visual illusions and their impact on your silhouette can help you camouflage physical irregularities and present a more pleasing image.

Silhouette—Beauty requires order. To present a beautiful image or what can be perceived as beautiful, your silhouette must be orderly, yet combined with interest. The line and cut of your clothes must suggest order to the mind of the beholder. In addition, balance is necessary. Balancing your silhouette creates a feeling of response, or projects a reassuring or stable quality. Lack of balance becomes a disturbing factor and suggests insecurity. A good example of the importance of line and balance in the silhouette of clothing is Jackie

Gleason. Jackie is a very stout man, but presents an excellent overall image by having his clothes tailored to balance—symmetrical silhouette. This clean, balanced look is accepted, and we are not attracted to the problem areas which his weight presents. However, in his characterization of the poor soul, in the *Honeymooners* TV show, his clothes are deliberately tailored to highlight his physical appearance. The straining jacket buttons, too tight pants, and too short sleeves immediately attract our attention as problem areas, which triggers our subjective judgment about his characterization's insecurities, frustrations, and ineptness. The same principles of line and balance apply to ourselves. If we have our clothes tailored to give us symmetry in line and balance, using visual illusion principles, we can camouflage our physical imperfections, rather than highlight them.

Physical Types

Generations of American men have been brainwashed into believing that certain patterns and fabrics are appropriate for certain physical types. For example, short men should wear striped patterns and avoid loud plaids. Tall men should wear patterns that accentuate the horizontal and avoid the loud striped suit, and ad infinitum. Consequently, tall men have avoided any type of stripe.

In reality, you must understand that there is only one hard fast rule in this area. *No one should wear any overdone or exaggerated pattern regardless of your physical type!* There are classic patterns and materials which can be worn by anyone. Using the principles of simplicity of line and balance to have your clothes tailored properly will allow you to wear any tasteful pattern no matter what your physical type. The short man may wear a subdued glen plaid tailored to balance and correct his silhouette with tremendous power. The tall man may wear a traditional muted stripe, again, tailored to give symmetrical and pleasing lines to his silhouette which make his height pleasing and reassuring rather than make him exaggerated and grotesque.

Tailoring a Silhouette

The motion picture industry discovered very early how important a man's silhouette was. Since the camera was an all-seeing eye which recorded images on a two-dimensional plane, lack of line and balance in a man's silhouette were magnified and accentuated to the point of grotesqueness. Wardrobe designers quickly discovered that an actor's physical imperfections had to be masked and hidden by his costume or clothing. The motion picture industry found that the silhouette was all-important. Consequently, they developed the science of line and balance to ensure that an actor's wardrobe gave him the right silhouette for the role he was playing. In addition, they could choose an actor for his ability and charisma, not for his height and build. They also understood that the mind sees what it expects to see when the image it receives is balanced and symmetrical in line. they concentrated on finding great faces, knowing they could package the actor through line and balance so that his physical imperfections would never distract.

Let's apply these principles to your physical type to better understand how you can use your silhouette to make your appearance more pleasing. Think in terms of balance and proportion rather than height and weight. For example, regardless of your height, you must keep your silhouette balanced with regard to the length of your legs and the length of your body trunk. Some men have long legs and short body trunks, while other men have short legs and a longer trunk.

Consequently, you must study your own silhouette and determine how to balance it with your clothing. Work with a good tailor who understands the principles behind balancing your silhouette. By standing sideways to the mirror you can determine approximately how proportioned you are. If you are long-waisted, your clothes must be cut to soften or camouflage. If you are a short-waisted person your clothes must be cut differently. Never think in terms of how each separate part of your body or silhouette looks, but rather how the entire picture is balanced. By concentrating on or camouflaging one minor problem, you find a solution which accentuates a major one.

For example, Alan Ladd, who was not much more than five feet tall, never wore a pin stripe suit, yet he filled the motion picture screen with power and projected the image of a man with no physical peer. In close shots between Ladd and a taller actress, Sophia Loren, for example, Alan Ladd would stand on a raised platform, yet his clothes were tailored so that he actually appeared taller than Miss Loren. The line and balance of his clothing conveyed the illusion of perfection so well that we assumed that he was tall, when in reality he was very short.

I first observed the power of the line and balance tailoring illusion while doing the "Festival of Lights" show at Madison Square Garden. Two major stars of completely different physical types—Cary Grant and Edward G. Robinson—were on the bill. I had the chance to observe them closely day by day. Cary Grant, a handsome man physically, understated rather than flaunted his power by a calculated simplicity in his wardrobe. He wore natural shoulder, two button suits in muted plaids for a traditional, established, quality look. He completed his dress with a white shirt, solid black tie, black wing-tip shoes, and black socks. His wardrobe was carefully underplayed to draw attention to Cary Grant, himself, not his clothes. The effect was overpowering. You felt that Cary Grant was physical perfection.

Edward G. Robinson always conveyed a strong physical image on the screen even though he was a very short man. At the "Festival of Lights" show, I watched Edward Robinson and Cary Grant on stage together, and realized there are no small men, but only those men whose appearance accentuates their lack of height. Mr. Robinson, in addition to being overweight, had short legs, short arms, no waist, and no neck. Yet he carried himself very well alongside Cary Grant. He was able to do this because his clothes were perfectly balanced, putting your subconscious mind at ease. You concentrated on Edward G. Robinson. You accepted his overall appearance by not being distracted by his height or the other physical shortcomings.

The Short Man

The short man's clothing problem is the same as everyone else's—make sure your clothes compliment you, the individual, not distract or highlight problem areas. Short men have the potential for wearing clothes extremely well. They usually possess good posture and a proud bearing. You dress so that all the right attributes are assumed. Simply remember line and balance to develop proper proportions. Edward G. Robinson and Jimmy Cagney, two of the shortest—yet best dressed—actors in Hollywood, developed certain wardrobe tricks which can benefit all men.

Although vertical patterns (classic stripes) have been traditionally recommended for the short man, any muted plaid or solid is also in order. Remember, balance your silhouette. Wear clothing which does not draw the viewer's attention. When wearing a sport coat and slacks avoid strongly contrasting colors, they tend to cut you in half and draw attention to your silhouette. Wear coats that are just long enough to balance your silhouette; consider carefully your body proportions to balance rather, than to attract attention. Jackets should be fitted to emphasize your waist. Here are four secrets not only for short men but everyone to be aware of:

1. The Disappearing Band Collar—Men with normal or short necks should buy disappearing band shirts. This shirt has no band under the collar and therefore sits down on the wearer's chest. This effect gives such men the illusion of a full or longer neck. You'll realize that the disappearing band collar will give you more height in your appearance.

2. Sleeve Length—Always be sure to show at least one quarter inch of shirt cuff below your sleeves. This glimpse of linen adds balance to your appearance, giving you the illusion of correct proportion.

3. Pants—You must have the waist, seat, and crotch area of your pants tailored for balance. The crotch area must come up to the last second before being uncomfortable. This will lengthen the area of light between the legs to emphasize the length of the legs. In addition, the width of the pant leg should be in proper proportion to the length of the leg.

4. Pants Length—Your pant leg should be fitted to the length of your leg. It should just touch without breaking the shoe top in the front and slant back one-half inch toward the top of the heel at the back. Avoid cuffs to give the illusion of more height for the short man. The tall man should also avoid cuffs for a much cleaner appearance.

The Thin Man

It's been said, "You can never be too rich or too thin." Maybe you never can be too rich, but you can surely be too thin to look good in your clothes. Remember, to balance your look wear jackets with just a trace of shoulder padding. Avoid to much shaping in the waist so that you don't accentuate your thinness. Wear vests—they will add extra bulk to your appearance. Thicker fabrics such as flannels and tweeds will give you more substance.

The Stocky Man

You must avoid the "bulging at the seams" look. Study the other areas on line and balance. Vertical stripes are helpful for you, although muted plaids and solids will also work. Smooth, thin materials are recommended, not heavy or tweedy materials. Neatness is extremely important. Avoid wide lapels and padded shoulders; aim for naturalness and balance. You may wear matching vests, but make sure they are not contrasting or fancy and that they cover belt buckles. Make sure your tie is long enough to reach your belt buckle. This lends balance and symmetry to your look.

The Tall Man

You must avoid the gawky "Ichabod Crane" look. The tall man can wear practically any classic pattern or color, as long as he does not deviate from the standards we've set. Plaids, checks, herring bones, or solids are all fine for everyone. You can mix colors—this cuts your height. You should choose jackets with two or three buttons and moderately rolled lapels. Trousers should be moderately full cut—

never wear skin-tight, low-slung trousers. The width of your trouser bottoms should be in proportion to the length of your foot.

In summary, the most important thing to remember about line and balance in your silhouette is that the brain attempts to put order into what it sees. Your job is to help this along by using your clothes as a visual illusion so that the brain observes order. You can accomplish this by studying your silhouette and having your clothes tailored to give balance and proportion to your silhouette.

13

SHIRTS

If the suit is the background or canvas upon which you package your appearance, the shirt is a versatile section of detail work in your image which can be used in a number of ways to convey subtle messages to those you meet. The color of the shirt can denote the nature of the occasion—white for more serious, blue for more casual. The collar, either straight or button-down, can provide the same type of signals. It's important to remember that you package yourself to say what you want in specific situations. For example, in a relaxed situation, a blue, button-down-collar shirt is much more reassuring than the white, crisp, straight point collar. As you read this chapter, analyze the shirts you need to present yourself the way you want in life.

An important point which must be stressed is that the shirt is as powerful a status indicator as anything you wear. You can ruin your entire image by having the wrong collar or wrong color shirt. Frayed collars or heavy stitching can totally destroy the image you desire to present. Consequently you must choose your shirts with utmost care.

After choosing a suit, you must then let that particular suit set the guidelines for selecting the accessories that complete your outfit. The suit itself determines the color of the shirt, ties, shoes, and belt. Suits in the blue, black, or gray family, or combinations in which those colors dominate, require a black shoe. Dark brown suits may be accompanied by either black or dark brown shoes. Tan suits are complemented by the dark brown shoe although black works well too. The belt must match the color of the shoe. You should choose shirts and ties for each new suit as you purchase them. The shirts and ties you already have seldom work as well as those chosen specifically for each suit. Remember, always choose number five and above suits for business. Consequently your business shoes will in most cases be black, and by brown shoes we mean only *dark* brown.

Shirt Materials

Your choice of shirting materials is relatively simple once you realize you must stick to the classics. The best shirt material is the cotton broadcloth. If you send your shirts to the laundry, you may buy the 100 percent cotton. If you prefer wash and wear you should buy the cotton-polyester blend for its durable press qualities. Be sure you always select blends with a larger percentage of cotton than polyester (55 percent cotton, 45 percent polyester, at the very least). This is necessary to avoid your collar fraying prematurely or having the collar material ball up around the neck. Here are the acceptable classic materials you should wear in a shirt.

Broadcloth—This preferred classic material not only wears the best, but says all the right things about you. The fine, close weave material works both in business and casual attire.

Oxford Cloth—this loose, basketweave material is somewhat more casual than the broadcloth, thereby lending itself more easily to non-vested suits and sport coats. Oxford cloth is a good classic and wears very well.

End on End—this is a material similar to Oxford Cloth except that there are colored threads interwoven with white threads. This shirt is particularly effective in pastels, since the white threads soften the colors of the shirt.

Batiste—Batiste is also a lightweight, luxurious material, used mostly for warm weather wear; however, because of its lightness it does not stand up well to laundering and lacks durability. This material should be worn only with a suit.

Jacquard and Pique—These are reserved for very dressy business or semi-formal occasions.

Collars

There are only four basic collars that you should wear.

1. The classic straight collar is recommended for all suits and sport coats and is a traditional favorite.

2. The tab collar, with or without the pin, is another classic favorite for suits—vested or unvested.

3. The Windsor collar has a wider spread and is frequently worn on custom or semi-custom shirts with a disappearing band to accentuate or lengthen the neck. This collar can be worn with vested or non-vested suits.

4. The classic button-down collar is recommended for everyday business and more casual wear in non-vested suits and sport coats.

You must remember that collar lengths should seldom vary from 3 1/2 inches. Otherwise, the collar becomes associated with a fad and is unsuitable. Avoid collars with heavy stitching, contrasting thread, noticeable button combinations, or large roll effects. Never wear a shirt with a contrasting collar unless you're in the glamour business. The double-knit or nylon shirt is completely unacceptable for you. Not only is it unmistakable, but it definitely evokes negative images. In addition, the spread of the collar should roughly correspond to the width of the shirt front shown and the cut or width of your lapel. Remember line and balance, and aim for symmetry in the entire area by being careful with the width of your tie knot.

Pockets and Fronts

You should avoid business shirts with pockets, unless your occupation requires that you work with your jacket off and carry pens or such in a shirt pocket. In that case, buy shirts which have no flap or button on the pocket. Never, never, never, wear a plastic pen and pencil holder in your shirt. If you want to command respect from those you work with. If you must wear pen and pencils, pick an expensive matched gold set, not cheap plastic pens. You will never be taken lightly with an obviously expensive pen and pencil set in your pocket. In addition, you will continue to broadcast success even though your jacket is off.

Choose shirts with either the fly or French front. Always avoid any exaggerated stitching or button configuration. If you are not immediately sure that it's a classic shirt, don't buy it. Simple elegance is the look you should strive for in your shirts. Make sure the shirts you buy have seven buttons down the front, so that the shirt will resist pulling out or apart around your belt area.

Taper and Cut

There are two or three different cuts available in dress shirts. They vary from manufacturer to manufacturer in name, degree of taper, and stylistic features. Your weight and body configuration will normally dictate whether you take a full cut, regular taper, or body shirt. If you tend to be heavy in the waist area, avoid the tapered look so that you don't appear to be straining out of your shirt. Leave the tapered look to the slim guys. Be careful, however, that your shirt doesn't bag, because it conveys an impression of disorderliness. When buying different brands of shirts, choose one at a time to see what the taper is like in that brand. When you find a brand that works, stick with it. Buy all your shirts in that brand, so that they all fit the same. "On Sale" is not the brand name for you. Neatness counts, with styling secondary.

Measurements

When you buy ready-to-wear shirts you only have two measurements to go by—the neck size and length of sleeve. Unfortunately, most men today have no idea how important these measurements are. The neck size is determined by taping your neck directly under the adams apple. Always round off your shirt size to the next half-size larger than the measurement. If the shirt is too tight, you'll reduce circulation, possibly causing headaches. The two largest veins in your body almost surface on your neck. If your collar creates pressure, much less cuts down circulation, by three o'clock in the afternoon you become tired, lose mental efficiency, and become nervous and irritable. However, if your neck size is slightly large, you simply tighten it up with your tie. Therefore, stay with the larger and more comfortable collar. Unbelievable as it may seem, the neck sizes on shirts also vary from manufacture to manufacturer. One brand's size 15 1/2 is generally different from another. Consequently, you must, again, buy one at a time, or find a store which has several shirts loose in assorted sizes and cuts for you to try on.

The sleeve length is determined by taping from the center of the yoke to a point extending slightly below the wrist bone, with your arms draping naturally alongside your body. Remember to periodically have your measurements taken because they will change slightly over your lifetime. In addition, both of your arms are seldom the same length, therefore you must buy your shirts using the size necessary for your longer arm. This may necessitate having the other sleeve shortened slightly.

Cuffs

There are only two shirt cuffs to be considered—the classic single button and the French cuff. All others may be disregarded as frilly and ostentatious. The cuff itself should be approximately three inches long. Anything else can be considered a fad and not appropriate. The shirt buttons should be of moderate size (no bigger than one-half inch) and plain white for the business and dress shirt. The French cuff is dressier than the single button, but is acceptable for all business occasions. Buttons on the sleeve vent are to be taken or left without fuss. They are inconsequential.

Monograms

The question of monogramming your shirts requires a little introspection on your part. Monogrammed shirts lend themselves more readily to certain industries and occupations. Study your contemporaries before you decide. Should you opt for the monogram, make sure it is simple, small, and tasteful. Avoid the ornate and distracting type. The monogram should be placed over the heart only. Monograms on the cuff or the waist in the European style are considered avant garde and showy. The smallest monogram legible is the recommended size.

Collar Stays

When buying shirts, check to see that they have removable collar stays. The stays should be removed before the shirt is laundered, so that pressing the collar doesn't leave an imprint in the crease around the stay or melt the stay itself. The best stays are plastic, so they may be bent or shaped as you like them. Collar stays vary in length. Don't hesitate to trim them down if they are uncomfortable or protrude into your neck making the collar stand up. Get into the habit of taking out the collar stays as you get undressed, keeping them with your wallet and watch for use the next day.

Colors

A great many men have difficulty choosing color combinations, pattern combinations, and coordinating their wardrobe correctly. One reason is that many men are tone blind if not color blind. Another is that they have been brainwashed into thinking that tricky combinations in color or pattern are to be aimed for. Finally, many men are talked into colors and combinations because they have little confidence in their own decisions. When choosing color and pattern combinations in shirts, ties, and suits, go for simple elegance by staying with the classic colors and patterns.

The "anything goes" period of fashion that was all the rage in the early 1970s is gone and good riddance. The riotous colors and exaggerated patterns have mellowed into subtle and sensible clothing with a grown-up and business-like appearance. Restraint is the guideline in choosing shirts, neckwear, and combinations. Harmony, not discord, is the look needed for success.

White is the most acceptable color for the business shirt. Ties may be matched to the suit or sport coat more easily when wearing white. Remember, white is your basic shirt color and is always appropriate. Pastel blues are the next favored business shirt, followed by ecru, which is a beige. Both of these soft colors are appropriate for most business situations. The solid shirt, of course, is the most versatile shirt, giving you flexibility in matching with ties and suits. If you must wear a stripe, wear only those listed below.

There are three classic stripes you may wear—university, candy, or the hairline or pin stripe. The background should always be white with the stripes being blue, burgundy or brown. No shirt should have more than two colors in it for business, and one of those must be white. Candy stripes, although casual, is one of the suggested stripes. The shirt should have button-down collars for sport coats and casual wear. As a general rule, the smaller and cleaner the stripe the more appropriate the shirt for business.

Small check shirts (tattersall, for example) are acceptable for some business occasions. When in doubt, don't wear them. These shirts must again only have two colors—white and the check. They should be worn with a solid tie only. More leeway is allowed in sport shirts, but again you should stick to the classic stripes, checks, and plaids. Avoid flowers, exaggerated designs of any type, or painted scenes. Again, by-pass the acetate body shirt which has definite negative connotations.

Made-to-Measure Shirts

Made-to-measure or custom shirts are becoming more and more difficult to find every day. With all their advantages, you would think that price would be the reason. In actuality, the made-to-measure shirt can be purchased for about the same price as a better ready-to-wear shirt. The real problem is two-fold. First, you must find a store which has a shirt manufacturer that follows instructions. Secondly, that store must have a salesperson who understands how to fit you and can communicate that fit to the manufacturer. By adhering to the following procedure, you should be able to find such a store. When you do, you are in for the treat of wearing a shirt that actually fits and looks like it.

First, check with your friends and acquaintances who buy made-to-measure or custom shirts. Make sure the shirts they are wearing are the classic, traditional look you want. Find out how long it took them to get the shirt made right, and who to deal with. Again, when you have sifted this information, choose one store and approach them dressed well to set the emotional climate necessary for them to desire your business. Next, you enter into negotiations. Explain that you realize that the minimum order is three or four shirts, but that you are reluctant to order that many until you are sure they will be made *right*. You will pay the extra charge for ordering only one shirt to ensure that first shirt is right before you order others. Since the made-to-measure shirt is seldom right the first time, it is easier to have one corrected, rather than three or four.

Now, looking over the shirting material, you pick out a

white broadcloth. Have your measurements taken, making sure that extra attention is paid to sleeve length, since they are seldom the same. By having your shirt sleeve lengths correct for each arm, you can subsequently have your sport coats and suit sleeves tailored to the correct length. Next, have the salesperson complete the measurements, having him pin up the shirt you are wearing so that you have an idea how the tailored shirt will feel when you receive it. Determine how close a body fit you want. Let comfort be your guide. Finally, specify length of the shirt body and tail to ensure they may be tucked in securely and won't creep out.

As I mentioned earlier, either the fly or French front is appropriate—simply a matter of personal preference. Cuffs may be French or regular, with the regular being a little more versatile (one button only, of course). Later, as you accumulate your shirt wardrobe, order a couple of French cuff shirts for dressier evenings.

The collar is vitally important to your preferred look. It is second only to your face as a focal point or center of attraction. I recommend for your test shirt you choose the plain collar. Remember, if you have a regular or short neck, order the disappearing band collar. If your neck is long, order the regular collar. Choosing the correct collar will give your shirt the correct fit as it lays on your chest.

Now that you have ordered your shirt, you must be patient yet meticulous. The shirt will arrive four to five weeks after your order. Try it on carefully. Make sure everything is exactly as you ordered it. If not, have the salesperson note the differences, and have the shirt returned for corrections. Continue the process until everything is correct. When that happens you are ready to order in multiples.

Stick with the same manufacturer as long as his quality remains constant. Develop a wardrobe of about a dozen custom-made shirts. Then, every Christmas, treat yourself to three or four more. The custom shirt that fits properly not only makes you look better but makes you feel better. In addition, you will be able to always buy the shirt you want, not settle for second-best because the color or size was not available. You buy shirts that you will wear, not ones you will ruefully discard later. Consequently, you will find that in the long run you save money.

As you can see, the shirt is a very important part of how you package yourself. We noticed earlier that incongruities in dress create suspicion in the minds of observers. Mismatched colors between shirt, suit, and tie not only suggest that you don't know how to match them, but make those who see you suspicious of you. A good example is an analysis of how you wear your shirt when your jacket is off.

When your jacket is removed, you can still retain some power and authority if your sleeves are buttoned and at wrist length. If you roll your sleeves up twice on the outside (the only way for a gentleman), this causes you to present a more casual, less authoritative presence. You will lose all credibility as a businessman if you have your sleeves rolled up on the inside. You will present a slightly shifty or evasive air. Finally, you will suffer a tremendous loss of power and authority if you wear short sleeves.

After analyzing what you want to say with your appearance, you can use this chapter on shirts as a guide to saying it.

Proper Shirts Can Save the Weekend

Too many of us use the summer season as the excuse to justify our sloppy or unsightly look. (Man, all week long I wear that straight jacket, shirt and tie. On weekends I'm entitled to some real comfort.)

Another man justifies his funny clothes by saying, "This is the way I save money. I buy what is on sale. This is how I do it. I buy good work clothes and cheap casual clothes."

This is not the way life works. Sooner or later you are going to bump into your boss, client or future prospect on a Saturday or Sunday. And you will strain your credibility with them. They will look at you and not understand what has happened. All week long you look one way, telegraphing all the positive attributes that give them confidence in dealing with you, secure in their judgment to depend on your advice. Now here you are saying one thing while your clothes are saying another. This is what social psychologists call a "conflict of expression." You have moved yourself back to square one and must start all over again to build confidence in that relationship.

Why not avoid this problem? Picking out casual outfits for after work and weekends, vacation and travel is easy, though it's hard to put into writing because of the variables in age, size, geographics and weather. Of course, stick with the idea of following a sensible budget. If you can afford more, great. Just stay with the same concept and get a little more expensive version of the same item.

Let's focus on sport shirts. The problem here is that most men buy them to draw attention to themselves. This is great folly, my friends. Those who really have the looks play them down. Can you conceive your CEO or President of your company wearing a red, green and yellow Hawaiian shirt or a rayon body shirt with lips all over it and a waterfall down one shoulder? Yet millions of these shirts are sold every year to men who yearn to be noticed and sought after—just like they're told in the ads.

For those who are building a solid wardrobe, start with the basic sports shirt that works at home, or travels to any part of the world and says all the right things about you.

It never changes, never goes out of style and just as important, works with everything and everywhere you go. We're talking about the cotton sport shirt. You will recognize it, as it never changes. It has one pocket on the left side (or over the heart) and has four buttons.

If you are able to afford it, start with four basic colors: blue, white, yellow and navy. These colors are solid. I repeat, solid, one color — no trimmings or odd color pockets, no initials, no nothing. The simplicity of the cotton sport shirt is what makes it classic — with one pocket that can be buttoned with a flap or not but only in one color. If you are 18 to 35, short sleeves are great. You can work them with slacks and a blazer for casual dining out or weekend parties and travel, plus wear them over shorts, Bermudas, bathing suits or pulled out over a pair of blue jeans. Every way you win.

Now if you are over 35, and want to be taken a little more seriously or feel you want to look a little more dressy, get the same kind of sport shirt material in long sleeves. This time it can button all the way down the front like a cardigan, both styles work.

But buy it in the same solid colors. These sport shirts will give you a complete sport shirt wardrobe at a minimum cost.

1.   2.   3.   4.

You must keep your silhouette balanced with regard to the length of your legs and length of your body trunk. These four men are all the same height but they have different body proportions. Number 4 has a long body trunk and short legs, while number 3 has a short body trunk and long legs. To balance their silhouettes both these men would take the same length of jacket. However, number 4 has been told that his jacket must cover his buttocks, so he buys a longer jacket which, while it does cover his buttocks, also accentuates the shortness of his legs to the point of caricature. Number 3, on the other hand, has also been told that his jacket should just cover his buttocks, so he buys a shorter jacket. This only exaggerates the length of his legs and makes him look like a scarecrow. As you can see in the diagram of these same four men below, both number 3 and 4 need the same length of jacket, regardless of where it ends with relation to the buttocks. Never think in terms of how each separate part of your body looks but rather how the entire picture is balanced.

pocket squares

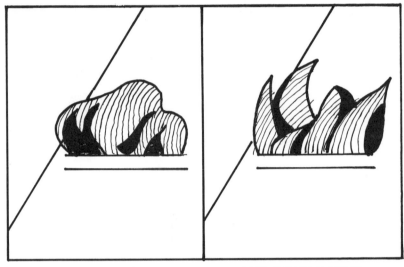

THE PUFF | THE FOUR-POINT

In composing the right package, one must pay attention to every detail — even the pocket handkerchief. Especially the pocket handkerchief. It can make the difference between being well dressed and <u>completely</u> well dressed. So, for our readers who want to add a definite panache to their appearance, I would like to offer these suggested styles of folding pocket squares.

THE FOUR-POINT FOLD. Lay the pocket square flat on a smooth surface. Pick up each of the four ends of the square and fold them in toward the center while holding onto all four points. Stuff into breast pocket with the points outward and adjust until you get the exact shape you want.

THE PUFF. The most formal (silk) style of all. Pick up the square in its center with the four points hanging down. Stuff into breast pocket leaving it wrinkled. Adjust until about 3/4" of wrinkled silk is showing.

(Note: Above examples are purposely exaggerated for graphic purposes.)

FOUR-IN-HAND   WINDSOR   HALF-WINDSOR

UNIFYING YOUR APPEARANCE WITH THE RIGHT KNOT

No matter which knot you prefer, you should know the three ways to knot a tie. Factors such as weight and texture of fabric, width and length of tie, your height, size of neck and shape of face must be considered. Take care to see that the front piece touches somewhere on the belt buckle Never vary more than one-half inch from the classic three and one-half inch width at the widest point.

Try tying a knot in the tie before you leave the store to ensure this is the right tie for you. Always use the index finger to put a dimple in the tie for symmetry.

Classic rain coats are always khaki or tan.
All raincoats and top coats should be at
least 3" below the knee. Sleeves should be
one to one and a half inches longer than
your suit coat sleeve.

THE TRADITIONAL
DOUBLE BREASTED
TRENCH COAT

THE RAGLAN SHOULDER
FRENCH FRONT (FLY FRONT)
EXECUTIVE RAINCOAT

The hallmarks of a gentleman's coat are always the same. This coat could be a camel, herringbone, chesterfield (just add a velvet collar) or cashmere, 100% wool or wool/poly in solid navy, black, gray or charcoal gray.

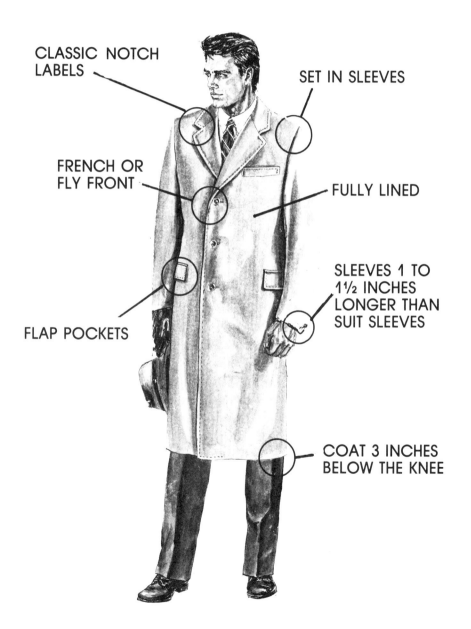

CLASSIC NOTCH LABELS

SET IN SLEEVES

FRENCH OR FLY FRONT

FULLY LINED

SLEEVES 1 TO 1½ INCHES LONGER THAN SUIT SLEEVES

FLAP POCKETS

COAT 3 INCHES BELOW THE KNEE

THE HALLMARKS OF A GENTLEMAN'S SUIT

Note How The Suit Sits Close to Neck.

Lapels are Rolled Low to Top Button. Never Pressed Flat.

No Excessive Bunching or Wrinkling.

Tapered Waist on Coat and Trousers. (Never to Extreme)

The Traditional Classic Outer Flap Pocket.

Real Bone or Horn Buttons. No Plastic Please.

Always ¼" of Linen Showing

Bottom Hem Even. No Sag, Expansion Pleat.

THERE ARE TWO
KINDS OF CLASS
IN THIS WORLD.
FIRST CLASS
AND
NO CLASS
THE CHOICE
IS YOURS!

There are basically two types of business shirts. The classic straight collar shirt, which is always done in broadcloth or pin point oxford. The classic button down shirt, which is done in oxford cloth, pin point oxford and broadcloth, and the formal tuxedo dress shirt, which is also made up in broadcloth. All three shirts come in 100% cotton and cotton/poly.

There are traditionally only four basic shirt collars for business.

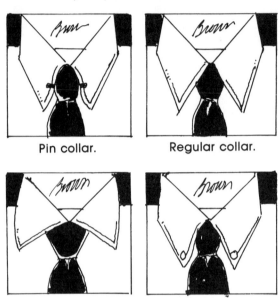

Pin collar.   Regular collar.

British spread collar.   Button-down collar.

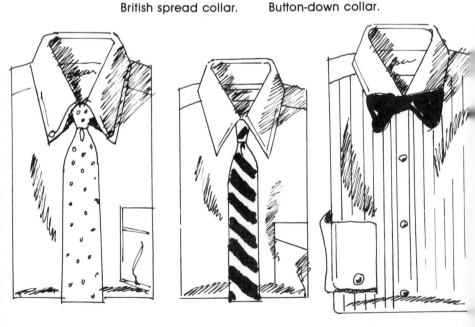

*"Give me a sincere tie. I'm on my way
to a very important meeting in my life."*
—Clark Gable in *The Hucksters*

14

TIES

Your shirt is the background of your tie. Since, as we mentioned earlier, your shirt should have no more than two colors, and one of those white, choosing ties can be made somewhat easier. In general, choose a tie darker than the suit; the contrast is sharp, crisp, and authoritative. Avoid color combinations that wash out or blend together; i.e., a pale blue shirt with a pale blue tie. Avoid patterns that clash. Don't try to subtly mix patterns. Trust instinct. If you are in doubt, don't try it. Instead, aim for classic, sharp contrasts. A plaid suit with solid white shirt and solid tie has the desired simple elegance.

The tie has often been referred to as the part of a man's wardrobe which signified his sex appeal. This can hardly be true, since national figures reveal that women buy 80 percent of the ties sold. As I explained earlier, a woman's motivation is different in buying than a man's. Consequently, ties bought for a man by the woman in his life do little to enhance him in the view of his business contemporaries. They are either cutesy, sexy, incredibly complicated, or unsuitable in color. Men forget that the tie is the single most important part of completing their wardrobe. They simply throw on any old tie for any number of whimsical reasons.

The tie is vitally important for a number of reasons. First, the tie and collar are second only to the face as a focal point or center of attraction. Second, the tie may be used to convey subtle messages about one's good taste and background. Third, the knot, pattern, length, and appropriateness of a man's tie are clues to his habits and character. They are as individual and revealing as his signature. Consequently the tie must be carefully selected with regard to material, color, and pattern. In addition, you must learn to tie the appropriate knot neatly to add line and balance to your outfit. The tie gives you the opportunity to complete your wardrobe to forcefully say all the right things about you.

Materials

There are several acceptable tie materials you should look for—silk, silk-polyester blends, wool, wool-polyester blends, and some all polyesters. The all-silk tie is the most versatile. It may be worn year-round and is found in patterns and colors to cover any occasion. Silk-polyester blends and the all-polyester blends which look and feel like all-silk are also found in many good colors and patterns. The real test is naturalness of look. If the synthetic or silk-synthetic blend doesn't look natural, you shouldn't wear it. Next are the wool and wool-polyester blends. Both have a dry, silk-textured look. Although limited in use to colder weather, both the knitted wool and wool challis ties are traditional favorites. Cotton, linen, and rayon are light weight warm weather ties, and, for that reason limited in function. All ties have linings which add body so that the tie may form a good knot and slip less. Be sure that the ties you choose do not have a lining too coarse to permit tying a good knot. Choose the material you like, which ties a good, slip-resistant knot, from the materials above. Try tying a knot in the tie before you leave the store to ensure this tie is right for you.

Knot and Length

There are several ways you may knot your tie. Since ties vary in length, you must take care to see that the front piece touches somewhere on the belt buckle. It is unimportant that the back be even with the front piece, simply that the front piece touch the belt buckle. Some men are either short or long waisted, which means that the back piece will vary in length after the knot is tied. If when the front piece touches the belt buckle, the back piece is the same length or shorter, then simply tuck it through the eyelet. If the back piece is longer, you tuck it through the eyelet or label and then either into your belt or fold it back through the eyelet. Nothing looks worse than having your tie length too short or too long. Both conditions indicate a lack of self-respect as well as a disorderly nature. Wear your belt buckle at a natural position, and have the tie end touch it.

There are three knots in use today which are acceptable— the four-in-hand, the Windsor, and the half-Windsor. The general rule to follow is to tie the knot relatively loosely and not to cinch it up too tightly. The knot should have a natural, unstrained look. Tied too tightly, or cinched up extremely, the knot conveys an impression of nervousness or uptightness in the beholder. On the other hand, a knot sloppily tied or loosened from the collar indicates either carelessness or too casual an attitude for most business situations. As always, neatness counts. The three knots are explained below:

Four-in-Hand—The four-in-hand knot is a neat, symmetrical, slightly elongated knot. This knot is especially recommended for bulkier (knits) or wider ties. In step one, leave the tie loose. Cinch the tie at the last step, using your index finger to put a dimple in the tie. The dimple is the final touch to complete an interesting cultured look.

Half-Windsors—The half-Windsor is the recommended knot for most ties. It is neat, symmetrical, and will not slip when used with most tie materials. The half-Windsor should be centered in the collar and again, use the dimple. This knot is usually more inviting to the eye and its elongated shape adds balance to the collar, neck, and facial area.

Windsor—The Windsor knot, although acceptable, is just not as crisp and business-like a knot as the half-Windsor. It may be used with ties of thinner materials for added bulk to the knot itself. The too bulky Windsor knot tends to distract and distort the crisp linear look of collar, tie, and tie length. If you feel you must use one, don't forget the dimple, center it correctly, and don't cinch it up too tightly.

The Width

There is a simple rule to follow regarding the width of your tie. Never vary more than one-half inch from the classic three and one-half inch width at the widest point. The classic look is always appropriate.

The Families

There are several tie families which you may employ to give yourself the correct look for business and social occasions. These are described below:

Challis—This tie is a traditional favorite. It is a lightweight, fine worsted fabric found in solids, patterns and printed designs.

Rep—This is a diagonally striped tie, made of silk, blends, or other fibers, woven in a corded, crosswise rib. These ties, with darker background, are dressy and excellent business ties.

Regimental Stripes—This is a rep tie, whose colors originally were those of British regiments or schools. Americans have adopted these ties for generations. They are fine for nearly all occasions.

Paisley—These are printed or woven designs found in silk and silk-polyester blends. To be safe, always lean toward the smaller, less intricate paisley.

Basketweave—This is a loosely woven wool found in solids, stripes, or plaids.

Club Ties—These ties are usually made of silk and silk-polyester blends. They are characterized by a dark background with a small insignia or design repeated in diagonal rows. This tie is a very acceptable tie as long as you opt for the smaller design or insignia.

Foulard—This tie is a twill weave of light weight silk or silk-polyester with small intricate printed figures. This is an excellent tie for business and informal occasions.

These basic families of ties are found in many colors, patterns, and designs. Other types are acceptable, but for our purposes let's stick to these classics. Given the wide range of variables available in the above families, you can find a tie for any occasion.

Patterns and Colors

Solid Ties—The solid tie is the most versatile in your wardrobe. It is found in several of the above families in many different colors. Avoid solid ties which have raised patterns, be they silk, silk blends, or whatever. Stick with the dark, richer colors, like maroon, dark blue, dark brown, or black. The solid tie may be used with any acceptable shirt described earlier, and any traditional suit material. Don't be afraid to wear a solid tie with a solid shirt and unpatterned suit. This combination highlights the richness of materials and colors used, as well as developing a clean, balanced look that is classic.

Striped-Ties—There are two diagonally striped patterns which you may wear successfully. These are the regimental and the rep described earlier. There are many variations in size of stripe and color which are acceptable, but you should stick to a dark background and crisp, sharply defined stripe for business. Smaller, more widely spaced stripes have a stronger, authoritative look than the regimental tie, which may be worn for business or informal occasions. In warmer weather you may choose a pastel stripe against a white background.

Patterned Ties—There are several different patterned ties which you may use. They are the club tie, the paisley tie, plaid tie, and the Ivy League or foulard tie. The club tie is usually an evenly spaced insignia, shield, or crest which is repeated against a darker background. The club tie pattern may also be a leisure activity symbol, such as a golf club or racing car, again repeated evenly spaced on the darker background. Generally, you should be sure that whatever is repeated on the tie is white, clear, and sharply defined. Otherwise, you'll find you are distracting others, since you notice them peering intently at your tie to see just what the design pattern is.

The paisley tie is an intricate, overall pattern which is either printed or woven, and resembles the pattern of cashmere shawls originally made in Kashmir. These ties are multi-colored patterns which can be used effectively to pick up an outfit. Just be careful you stick to more conservative subdued classics. The paisley is not a serious, business tie, but rather a more relaxed, sporty tie.

The plaid tie has a box-like design consisting of horizontal and vertical stripes criss-crossing in several colors. This tie is another tie which is not suited for serious, business negoti-ations; however, it has some merit in less formal situations. Stick with heavier woolen patterns in classic colors.

Another traditionally accepted tie is the foulard tie or Ivy League tie. This pattern generally consists of small multi-colored designs (triangles, concentric circles, dotted dia-monds, or ellipses) against a darker background. It is referred to as the Ivy League tie because of its original popularity with the northeastern university students. These are versatile, widely accepted ties which can be worn for business, semi-formal or informal activities depending on their colors.

Polka Dot and Diamond Tie—The polka dot and diamond patterned ties are both versatile, acceptable ties. The polka dot is generally found with a dark background and white dots. The size of the dot varies; however, smaller dots are dressier. You should pick dark blue, maroon, or brown back-grounds with white dots. These ties make for a crisp, sharp effect on white shirts in almost any pattern suit. They are acceptable for business, semi-formal and informal wear.

The patterned tie is similar to the polka dot. Also very versatile, it is acceptable for all occasions.

Unsuitable Ties

You should stay with the ties I've described above. With the wide variety of colors and patterns available you can find a tie for any occasion. You must avoid ties which are unusual in color and pattern. Geometric shapes, hand-painted pictures, pastoral scenes, etc. are all taboo. Stay away from the hybrid tie which may be polka dot in one area and striped at the bottom. Avoid very light colored pastels, except for the silver or white tie worn for semi-formal wear. Stay with the classic, traditional size, shape, and colors. Avoid the embroidered tie with the raised patterns.

Bow-Ties

Although bow-ties are seen less frequently today, some men wear them very well. In general, you may consider the bow-tie a less serious tie. Unless you have established a business identity for yourself associated with always wearing a bow tie, don't wear them for serious business occasions. Again, stay with the classic, traditional bow-tie.

A continuing theme throughout our discussion of packing is consistency. If you are inconsistent in your approach to the image you present you either look ridiculous, suspicious, or just plain careless. None of these is the look you need to achieve your goals in business or pleasure. The tie can either be the perfect touch of success packaging or the unsettling disruption which makes a Krakatoa of your image. If you have trouble matching patterns then stay in the company of Cary Grant, Sidney Poitier, and Henry Ford, who always wear solids. You could do a lot worse.

The Right "Cover"

How to Select an Outer Coat to Complement a Classic Wardrobe

Our previous articles have covered many of the correct basic components of the proper business wardrobe, or, as we've referred to it, your personal "package." As with any package, there's a right outer wrapping for yours, specifically coats and/or outer wear. They are an important investment, both in appearance and cash.

Topcoat or overcoat?

Today's world is one of almost totally controlled indoor temperatures. For outdoors, where temperature is a factor in clothing selection, there has evolved a more sensible approach to achieving comfort while preserving good taste. By now, most people are aware that several layers of lightweight clothing have proven to be as effective in providing warmth as yesterday's heavy and bulky overcoats. Also, refinements in weaving techniques have produced excellent fabrics of warmth without weight. The net result is a growing trend to a more universal use of the topcoat, even in colder climates. Whichever you choose—topcoat or overcoat, it's the cut and styling to consider first—weight of fabric is optional.

The right topcoat styles

There are four classic coat styles to consider when selecting an outer coat for business.

The most formal of the four is the Chesterfield. This

"gentleman's" coat is an excellent all-around coat for business as well as dress occasions. The classic Chesterfield is a fitted coat with distinctive lines. Properly made, it's an excellent choice to help create balance in your silhouette. Traditional colors are navy, brown and medium to charcoal gray. Number one fabric is herringbone. Solids may also be worn.

A less formal choice is the Polo coat. Because it is generally done in camel's hair, or camel-colored fabric, the style is also referred to as the Camel coat. Usually double breasted (though not necessarily) the styling over the years has remained as consistent as the fabric. Its distinguishing feature is a half-belt in the back, NOTE: Another version of the Polo coat, which is a wrap-around with a full-self belt tied around the waist, is strictly casual; very smart for leisure wear — totally unacceptable for business.

Another of the "big four" basics is the British Army or British Warm Coat. This old standard originated in World War I. Despite its being one of the lesser known, it is nevertheless a true classic. As the name indicates, it's a military style, double breasted, with epaulets and usually made of wool melton, a cloth woven in England. It's a tough, closely woven fabric that travels well and provides exceptional warmth. It's a wise investment only for the man who lives or travels extensively in very cold, damp climates.

Probably the most widely accepted of the four styles is the Raglan Coat. It takes its name from its distinctive sleeve. Instead of the standard set-in sleeve, the Raglan has a seam that extends diagonally from the underarm to the neckline. This design feature makes it extremely popular for its easy fit and comfort, plus the ease with which it slips on over even the bulkiest clothes. Its being less closely fitted makes it important to check details that provide a well-tailored look. Be sure that the armholes are smoothly seamed for a nicely finished feeling.

Raincoats

With only two types to consider, decisions here are easy.

As in the topcoat category, the Raglan shoulder, French front executive raincoat is the first and best choice. Watch the top men in large companies. Most of them favor this style.

The other choice is the Trench coat. First worn by British officers in the trenches and on the battlefields of World War I, its styling has remained virtually the same since. At its inception, every feature of the coat had a practical purpose. The gun flaps shielded the shoulder from rifle kickback; the shoulder yoke gave added protection from the rain; the inverted pleat or riding wedge at the back enabled the wearer to walk fast, run, or ride horseback comfortably. While the need for some of those features no longer exists, the details stay the same. In its authentic form, the trench coat is a good choice for business, adding a certain dash to your appearance. Skip things like brass buttons, hand grenade holders, or any jazzy extras.

Whether you choose trench coat or raglan, remember these essentials:

Stick with a classic khaki tan—no exceptions.

Wear the right length. The raincoats should be at least three inches below the knee, never above. Very slight deviations may be considered to improve line and balance.

Sleeves should be one to one-and-a-half inches longer than your suit coat sleeve.

Final Coat Notes

These are some general points to check in selecting a topcoat:

It should slip on comfortably. Whether raglan or set-in sleeve, it should be fully lined to achieve that end.

Check the collar. It should hug your neck, fitting snugly right on top of your suit collar.

Button up! Check the hemline and sleeve length for changes in length or just to even it up. Attend to alterations before you take the coat out of the store.

On With It

Believe it or not, all of the above items can be affected by the way you put your coat on, so here's our final tip:

When putting your coat on, hold each sleeve of your suit coat as you slip into your outer coat. That prevents their bunching up in the outer coat sleeve. Then, holding the collar of the top coat at the back of the neck with one hand, reach up under the back of the outer coat, grasp the bottom of your suit coat at the center back. Pull UP on the coat collar and DOWN on the suit coat. With both hands on the coat lapels smooth it out. This should "seat" the suit on your neck while setting the top coat in place over it, so that both hug the neck.

Gloves: but not golden
Keep them simple; keep them leather

The trick to having good clothes is, first, to think about how they are going to be used before purchasing them and, second, once they have been purchased, to take care of them.

You should always think of a one-time purchase when you buy gloves. If you take care of them and wear them only for the reasons you bought them, They will wear for many years.

For the businessman who is packaging himself, gloves must

complement the outfit he is wearing. Good gloves are priced from $12.50 to $150.00, depending on material, label, and quality. Inside linings vary from cashmere to real fur, from polyester to none at all. A business executive should not even consider heavy-lined gloves. With his camel-hair coat or British Warm topcoat, he should wear a simple pair of pigskin gloves, lined or unlined as he chooses. A pair of dark solid leather gloves would also be appropriate. Solid black leather gloves should be worn with the dark navy or gray topcoat. For the man who has a full social life, a pair of gray suede gloves, strictly for that area of his life, would be another sound purchase.

In choosing gloves for the business world, remember that they should not attract any attention. They should never be purchased with the idea of their being a conversation piece. There should be a feeling of unobtrusive quality in each pair. Never buy a pair of gloves with trick combinations or contrasting color stitching to draw attention to them. Like your other accessories they complement your package.

Once you move on to more casual or rural areas of the country, you can buy part-leather or part-knit gloves to be worn with your car coat or all-knit gloves for pure warmth where needed. Obviously, the colder the weather, and the longer you must be in it, the warmer the gloves you need.

Once into the casual area of life, don't succumb to anything in the way of bright, gaudy gloves. Try always to stay in one color only, and the fewer jazzy zippers and/or buttons the better.

The color of the gloves is determined by the color of your coat. Try to stay in one color family, then you can mix and match outfits and gloves. When not in use, take the gloves off carefully, then fold softly together and put them into the inside pocket of your coat . . . deep down in the inside of the pocket where they'll be safe (and not fall out) till the next time you need them.

Off on the Right Foot

When you consider the cost of your shoes today and that your foot hits the floor 7,000 times a day; that walking one mile exerts a pressure of 500,000 pounds on your feet and the average person walks the equivalent of twice around the world in a lifetime; it is time we realized the importance of putting some serious forethought into buying our shoes.

If you can manage it, you should have at least three pairs of shoes for business; not only do shoes last longer if they are allowed a rest between wearings, but several pairs also add variety to your wardrobe and comfort. And when you come home from work, take them off and put them away. These are your "work shoes" that you wear to make money. Slip into casual shoes for casual time.

Black is the color of authority, and can be worn with any color. It is mandatory for grays, blues, and black and can even be worn successfully with dark brown or tan. If you wear brown suits and want brown shoes, keep them dark brown. If they are light tan, have them stained dark brown.

You need two pairs of lace-up shoes, either wing-tip or plain toe. The message of the lace-up shoe is subtle, reassuring the observer's subconscious about your dependability. You obviously took more time getting dressed than did the man who slipped into a pair of loafers.

Classic dress slip-ons are acceptable, but avoid suede loafers, boots, heavy buckles, platforms, riotous colors or shiny plastic. Plastic not only looks phony, but like the cordovan shoe, lacks the breathing capacity of leather. Because your feet perspire, eventually they are going to give off odors.

When you shop for shoes you should pay even more attention to fit than you do to style. You will spend around two thirds of your life in your shoes and nothing can drain away your energy faster or leave you more tense and irritable as quickly as a pair of shoes that does not give the proper support.

A suit can be altered but a shoe that bites or blisters will bite or blister as long as you wear it.

Because both feet are seldom the same size, try both shoes on and walk around in them before you buy. Find a store staffed by professionals who know shoes and understand proper fit. The shoe salesman who asks you for your size instead of measuring it for you is likely to send you home with a pair of shoes that does all the wrong things for your feet. Although sizes have been standardized, there is still variation from manufacturer to manufacturer.

If you are over 35 or prone to swollen feet, don't buy shoes when you are tired or late in the day. A shoe fitted to even a slightly swollen foot is never going to feel right.

Shoes should break just at the joint of the big toe. If the break is farther back, the shoe is too long and is going to blister your feet.

When you stand, there should be enough room between the end of your toes and the end of your shoes. Your arch should fit snugly against the arch of the shoe. If you have to force your foot down to meet the shoe, it's too narrow. And it's too wide if there is too much space on either side of the instep. The heel should grip your foot firmly so as not to slide up and down when you walk.

Finally, even if the shoes are a good fit, don't press your luck. Wear a pair of shoes for brief intervals until they are completely broken in.

If you seem to be particularly hard on your shoes, if the

heels run over quickly or the inner side of the shoe slants down, you might consider a medical check-up. Your problem may only be poor posture or a peculiarity of your walk, but it could also point to a back or spinal irregularity that is correctable through exercise.

Proper care can prolong the life of any shoe. First, always polish a new pair of shoes before wearing them. It protects the leather and makes them easier to shine in the future.

Your shoes will keep their shape longer if you put shoe trees into them between every wearing. Wooden trees are best because they absorb moisture from damp, sweaty, shoes.

Always use a shoe horn to protect the heel of the shoe—and your own heel—from unnecessary strain.

Metal taps fixed to the toe end of the sole help prevent wear. Never let the heels wear down too far. It throws the shoe off balance and looks sloppy.

Paste and cream are the best polishes to produce a long-lasting shine and to nourish the leather. It's a good idea to clean your shoes with saddle-soap about every fifth shine. This cleans away the old polish and keeps the leather soft, and prevents it from cracking.

Formal Without Frills
Selecting a tuxedo that will stay in fashion

Let's assume you've assembled the perfect business wardrobe. You have the right suits, sport coats, pants, shirts, ties, shoes, socks, etc. Careful planning has provided you with the necessary elements for all your business activities and much of your leisure. The fabrics, the cut, the fit and color coordination are everything they should be. You're well dressed and you know it! You have the right image for a successful career. So what's left to discuss?

Well, let's make one more assumption: your social life style has changed as you've become more successful. So, chances are there will be occasions when even the most versatile dark business suit won't fill the bill. Invitations to more and more functions specifying "Black Tie." If your business and/or social life requires that you wear a tuxedo three or more times a year, you should own one.

Rentals are fine for the one-formal-function-a-year man. Rental is the ideal answer for the high school student who needs a tux once a year at prom time. For the student, there are the problems of his fast-changing physical measurements and his underdeveloped fashion philosophy. He very likely wants a tuxedo that suits his current taste. NOT one like his father's! For him, investing in a tuxedo is highly impractical. For high school students and even some young collegians, simply recognizing the need to "dress for the occasion" is a major step in the direction of wardrobe awareness. Often, the first personal fashion statement a young man makes is his choice of tuxedo for his first formal party.

At every age, every man looks good in a tuxedo. Whether you own or rent — there are simple guidelines to follow, in either case, but especially when investing in your own, think in terms of the long haul. The more traditional you stay, the longer life your tux will enjoy.

For color, there are only two to consider: black and midnight blue. Pass up colors, brocades, iridescents, etc.

Fabric should be light-weight wool worsted or a polyester-wool blend for year-round use. Remember, you'll be wearing this suit indoors, dancing, dining, sitting, etc. These light-weight tux pants will work fine in summer (or sunny climates) with a white dinner jacket. About white jackets: your geographical location or travel habits may determine the practicality of owning one as opposed to renting. One common objection to owning one is the tendency for the white to turn dull or "yellow." A little-known preventive measure is to store white apparel in BLACK garment bags or wrapped in BLACK tissue paper.

Now we're ready for tuxedo styling. Single breasted jackets are best. Double breasted, while technically considered a classic, tends to come in and go out in favor on the fashion scene. Choose the natural shoulder jacket. Its good taste transcends yearly fads. For the same reason, you'll be wise to stick with a center vent. Side vents also tend to be "in" or "out" at the whim of fashion.

There are three acceptable basic collar choices. They are the shawl collar, peaked lapel, and standard notched lapel. Again, one, the notched collar, tends to be the most constant. Keep lapels close to 3 1/2" wide. Lapels should be covered in either of two fabrics, satin or grosgrain. Both are fine though satins are more traditional.

Pocket flaps on the jacket are preferred, but straight piped pockets are very acceptable. Avoid patch pockets.

Pants are straight legged, always the same color and fabric as your jacket (except, of course, when wearing a white dinner jacket). Side seams are finished with braid, grosgrain or satin stripes. No cuffs!

You may wear a separate cumberbund, or choose a waistband on the trousers to match the fabric in the lapels.

Tuxedo accessories are simple and classic. Your shirt is white with a choice of box pleated or pin-tucked bib front, with French cuffs. The wing collar is a dashing touch for the young man. The conservative man sticks to the regular shirt collar.

Cuff links and studs can be pearl or plain gold or black onyx. Any additional ornamentation is a detriment. Keep it simple.

Wear a silk bow tie of the same fabric as your lapels. A good clip-on is fine, although it's fun once you learn to tie one correctly.

Proper shoes are a must. Patent leather is right in either of two styles. The pump with flat bow on the instep is correct with tuxedo or tails. Generally, for "black tie," laced patent shoes are more popular. Keep them looking great for years by storing them on wooden shoe trees.

Socks, of course, could be a light silky solid black over-the-calf style.

As we mentioned in our coat article, the best outer wear for formal use is a single-breasted Chesterfield with velvet collar. Here, again, black or midnight blue is best.

Formal evenings are very special, no matter what your age. There's one way to guarantee you the poise to be at your best for these times. Have the proper tux and accessories, and have a great time!

Wedding Pictures for Fond Memories

Inside every human is a desire to share, to support, and be supported by emotion. We like stability.

A study by the Marriage and Family Counseling Center of Purdue University indicates that approximately 96 percent of us get married sometime in our lives, and the number grows each month. The director of the institute says, "People fundamentally need relationships with other people. As long as this need exists, there will always be marriage."

We all think of June as the month of weddings. But studies have shown not only that marriage is a year-round phenomenon (with monthly percentages extremely close), but that marriage is on the increase as well. More and more people opt for marriage and choose to celebrate it in a beautiful formal rite. So, the possibilities for creating the perfect and individual wedding have grown proportionately.

The first concern of the bride-to-be is her trousseau and the ensembles for her bridesmaids, her mother and the grooms' mother. There are two great magazines to buy or write to for more information for the women: *Modern Bride* and *Bride*.

The choice of the ensembles for the groom, best man and ushers depends on the time of day and the formality of the wedding. For a formal affair before 6 p.m., the cutaway is appropriate. After 6 p.m., formal tails or a semi-formal tuxedo does the job. In the summer, a white formal jacket replaces the tuxedo jacket. For informal weddings, a dark blue or dark grey suit is fine.

Your wedding is one of the most beautiful and emotional times in your life. At that moment the dreams and expectations of the bride and groom are at their zenith.

You hire a photographer to capture the day so you can remember it throughout your lives. Your parents will bring out these photos hundreds of times to relive each one of them with their friends, neighbors and business associates. Ten years down the road, your children will be bringing out your wedding pictures and showing them to their friends. And, of course, one day your daughter or son will show them to their prospective mates, and so on.

And what will these pictures say about you? Are you the super-dude with shaggy sideburns and handlebar mustache? Is your hairdo so bouffant and perfect that people wonder if you were late for your own wedding, fixing your hair? Does your tuxedo look like the latest fad that year when zoot suits were in?

If so, 20 years from now, when you and all those other people look at the pictures, you will die inside. And to think you paid good money to perpetuate your modest background so everyone will know. It's like the local doctor having his high school grades published and everyone finding out he flunked first aid.

But this needn't happen. You can package the whole affair in style. Wear a classic tux, tails or a cutaway. Always stay on the conservative side. No ruffles in the shirt (white shirt only). No pastel tux. And take a good look at your shoes (the camera probably will). Wear black patent leather lace-up or conservative slip-ons.

Now, the moment of decision. Stand in front of the mirror and look at your hair and sideburns. Project yourself 20 years into the future — you're a successful businessman in a position of responsibility. You have many people under you. Think of how you will look to those people. The man who wears his hair in a moderate cut and doesn't radically change his hairstyle never seems to age, and old photographs of him never look out of style.

With age, men earn distinction, learn to cope
Anonymous

15

LET ELEGANCE BE YOUR GUIDE

You're not getting older; you're getting better. This Madison Avenue cliche has taken on an entirely new meaning as the mature gentleman assumes more responsibilities, more obligations and therefore more pressure. Never shrink away from the years; be proud of them.

A wise man said it all when he said, "Youth is a gift of Nature; Age is a work of art."

I love the story about Elizabeth Taylor, who when she was asked if she worried about the crow's feet on her face, answered, "Hell, no. I earned every line on my face."

If a sex goddess can face the ravages of time with such candor and courage, it's time we made those years pay off for you too.

We graciously call it maturity. It is that look that says, "I've met life on its terms and survived."

Age alone does not bring wisdom but age does bring experience. It is that look that a man has developed as the years come and go. It is a gracious acceptance of life's lessons, the good along with the bitter, happiness along with tears. It is the look not only of experience, but of pride and self-respect. His age has given him a look that when you look at him you know—he has coped with emergencies, disappointments and confusion.

And has brought balance to his work.

He has passed all his adolescent turmoil and youthful frustration.

He can recognize the difference between the situations he can do something about and the situations he can do nothing about.

He has reared his family and they are grown or nearly grown. Now he and his wife can broaden their area of life as they see fit.

He may have lived in a number of communities and probably has good friends where he lived.

He has the years that have taught him patience. If necessary,he is ready for the long haul needed for real results in business.

He has long experience in budgeting time and money.

He can recognize the shortcomings and pitfalls of pettiness in business, how to avoid it, or if necessary how to cope with it.

He has learned to win and to pay his dues. He has proven it by paying them.

He stands now before God and we know he did the best with what he had when he was called upon to do it.

Age gives dramatic license. It allows him to make certain judgments. For instance, the mature man can wear:

white linen handkerchief
bow ties
a mustache
family rings
watch fob with his watch
a boutonniere
a cane
a contrasting vest, in taste, of course

He can, if he likes, drive older cars or smoke cigars without looking affected.

The '60s brought back a lesson we seem to have forgotten. Youth is wonderful but is not to be confused with experience. Life is not only knowing two plus two equals four, but knowing what four means.

Leather Accessories for Businessmen

Your belt and wallet are opportunities to add the rich texture of fine leather to your appearance. Your belt should always match the color of your shoes — either dark brown or black. Pick one of medium width, with a square or round shaped gold or brass buckle. Avoid ornate, large or complicated belt buckles; they distract from and unbalance your overall image. Belts for sport clothes can be of material other than good leather, but stick to basic colors and classic materials.

Most men put a lot of pressure on the belt buckle and, consequently, on the belt holes. A belt will wear only so long under such pressure. Do not wear an old, tired-looking belt with stretched, worn belt holes. Recognize when it's time for a new belt.

A wallet sometimes becomes an old friend to a man, and

he cannot bear to part with it. He loads the wallet with all his confidences, carries it long past its prime and fails to notice signs of age or flaws in the wallet. But to make the right impression of businesslike efficiency, you will have to part with the timeworn friendliness of a tattered wallet. Replace your wallet with a more functional pocket secretary and card carrying case.

Your wallet for business should be the thin, oblong, pocket-secretary type in dark saddle-brown or black leather. Never wear a wallet in your back pocket. Carry it in your inside jacket pocket.

Choose a pocket secretary for function, not for flashy detail. Gold lettering, embossed edges and monograms are unnecessary and gaudy. Carry your personal cards and credit cards in a small card carrying case in your suit coat side pocket. It should be leather and the same color as your pocket secretary.

Once you have found them, don't ruin their shape by overloading them. If a pen fits easily within the pocket secretary have one for convenience sake. When shopping for it, just remember the pen should be thin, gold and functional—and keep it clean.

Your secretary and card case will accumulate the normal, everyday collection of cards and notes, which must be removed periodically to a proper storage place. Don't let the papers accumulate until they bulge or display disarray when you bring it out to pay a bill or write a memo.

A pocket secretary is not a photo album. You should sit down tonight and remove everything in it and analyze it. Put back only the things you really need. Keep the credit cards that you use on a daily basis in your card case. No one is impressed by seeing your 10 different gas credit cards. One or two pictures of the family is all right, but anything more is a bore. Cash should be carried in your side pants pockets.

Watches Tell More Than Time

Classic clothing has always combined balanced elements to achieve an elegance of line. This is carefully orchestrated by those people who understand their individual look and what they are trying to accomplish with it. All parts of your clothing work together so that the eye of the observer is not distracted by the width of your lapels, the depth of your cuffs or the length of your jacket. The eye moves easily over balanced elements sensing their harmony as a symmetrical silhouette.

Once you have established this feeling with your clothing, don't let your jewelry and accessories interfere. When you are accessorizing a quality look think in terms of enhancing order with interest.

For our purposes, the jewelry and other accessories you wear are considered items of interest even if they are functional. Your major pieces of clothing establish order. Certainly you want your jewelry to provide interest, but for business, you keep the complexity of its design very low, for maximum aesthetic value. For business the simpler the jewelry the better.

To understand the relationship between interest and order, consider the following three mental pictures.

The first picture is a man wearing a classic traditional vested suit standing there looking at his wrist watch. It represents pure order, unadorned. In the second, interest is added by a classic gold wrist watch with an unobtrusive black leather strap, and black Roman numerals on a white face. A white linen pocket handkerchief is correctly folded in his lapel pocket. However, by keeping basic classic accessories simple, the order established by the clothing is not cluttered.

In the third picture, the accessories are more complex.

There are little tricky innovations that cause attention and their complexity is distracting, decreasing the overall balance and order of the image presented.

Let understated elegance always be your guide in accessories. Expense is not a guide. Many expensive pieces may not be tasteful. Also your accessories should be functional rather than frivolous.

Your watch should tell what time it is, not the barometric pressure in London, or the current phase of the moon. And think twice before you buy a watch that requires you to press a button to learn the time of day. What possible reason would an intelligent business man have for tying up both hands just to find out what time it is? That maneuver just makes you look as if you had extra time on your hands at best.

Think a minute! Can you describe the kind of numerals and face your friend's watch has? If you can, he may be wearing the wrong kind of watch. Avoid tricky details like colored watch faces, elaborate dials or hands or fancy numbers.

The watch you need for business is a thin gold watch with a plain classic face and a dark wrist band. Anything else, any eye catching details, will detract from and clutter your image.

For your pleasure time, business entertaining, or more formal wear, use one of the beautiful gold classic watches defining another part of your life. It will immediately move you into a tasteful sophisticated elegant look.

Start thinking about your next watch purchase. Every time you look at your watch, so does everyone else. It tells a lot more about you than the time.

Handkerchief Folding is Easy, Adds Dash

If you have come to the point in life where you are a little tired of seeing the same old you in the mirror every morning, let's look at a very easy way to add dash to your appearance. Get a handkerchief—just a white handkerchief. Cotton or linen is your best choice for a business or conservative look. For more panache, use a silk square (more on that later). Once you have folded it correctly, you can use it for months and have a clean, fresh look. Every so often, take it out and refold it or adjust it to its proper position in the suit pocket.

Obviously, the pocket handkerchief is not for cleaning glasses or the nose. Maintain its soft, puffy, rolled look. If you flatten it out, it takes on an old tired look, which draws attention to the problem.

The golden rule here is, if you are not sure a handkerchief is right for you, don't use it. No one is going to walk up and say: "You're not wearing a handkerchief." Think of a handkerchief as a smart woman thinks of her jewelry: "a little touch of class."

In considering a silk square, remember they are for evening entertainment, pleasure time or sophisticated business entertaining. In purchasing your handkerchief and/or silk pocket square, pick one with a hand rolled (not machine hemmed) edge. Remember to regularly launder and starch your white handkerchiefs.

The white handkerchief goes with every tie and suit. The silk pocket square must never match the tie. Always take the darkest background color of the tie and choose a solid pocket square in that color.

There are four basic ways to fold your handkerchief. The four-point is the most popular for the linen and the puff for the silk pocket square. Again, it is the soft, full look of elegance —not the flat look—that is preferred.

For the four-point, open the handkerchief and lay it out flat before you. Pick up the center, where all the creases meet, with your right hand. Close your left hand around the cloth below and draw the handkerchief through it with your right hand. Bring all four corners together. Fold the handkerchief in half and stuff it into the breast pocket, leaving the point not more than 1/4 inches over the pocket.

The next most popular style is the puff. This is the reverse of the four-point. For the puff, go through the same motions as the four-point, but fold the points halfway up the handkerchief. Stuff the handkerchief into the pocket with the points down and the rounded end—the puff—upright.

The roll is another popular, but conservative, style. For this, lay the handkerchief out flat and fold it in half, into a rectangle. Roll the folded, long, side up to the edges of the handkerchief. This will leave you with a long tube. Fold that in half and stuff into the pocket, leaving the ends as loose as you see fit.

The petal looks slightly different from the four-point. Fold the handkerchief into a square, then into a triangle and, if size permits, into another triangle. Stuff the end with the folds into the pocket, leaving the loose edges sticking out over the lip of the pocket. Adjust the edges to look casual.

For the man who only wants a handkerchief in his pocket: Take a handkerchief, fold it in half once again, and leave a straight line of white, or whatever, across the top of the pocket. Now sit down and think how you want people to notice your handkerchief—because they surely will.

Classy Suede Should be Classic

Most of us at one time or another have worn suede. It is a strong, supple leather that was brought to France from Sweden in the 15th century. In America's early frontier days, it was the settlers' favorite garb.

Although suede is strong and durable, it requires special care.

The name suede refers to the velour finish that comes from buffing an animal's hide. It is genuine leather that has been turned inside out and given a velvety nap. The hide of each animal used for suede, whether it's lamb, sheep, pig or goat, has unique skin markings, texture and weight. This, of course, is no measure of quality. Trying to judge the best quality of two suede coats is like choosing between two fine cars. It is a personal choice.

The important choice here is style. The further away the style is from the classic sport coat or jacket, the shorter the amount of time you will be able to wear it fashionably. That's why when you see the "sale" sign, watch out for tricky styles and cuttings that have already seen their day. The suede jacket or coat is a great item to wear when it is bought correctly and cared for properly.

Here are a few suggestions for your suede garment:

Never wear it over anything soft or light when you first purchase it. Suede residue, also known as "crocking," is natural for new suede and will disappear after a few wearings. It is important to remember that "crocking" is a characteristic and not a fault of suede. It is due to the emery buffing a garment receives at the factory. To eliminate this problem, rub with a dry towel and avoid wearing light colors with darker shades of suede the first few times you wear the garment. It will soon be gone.

Never place or store leather in plastic bags. Always use good hangers (wishbone or padded) to hang suede apparel, and cover them with a cloth wrapper. Any kind of animal skin must be allowed to breathe when stored or it will dry rot, discolor or even fade.

Never store anything that is made of leather in a hot attic or a damp cellar. It will mildew or rot. Of course, this rule also applies to any of your leather luggage or other leather items. Even if it is a dry place for storage, never store garments when they are stained or soiled. Moths tend to nibble little tracks in the nap of the suede. Before you put them away in storage, make sure they are all cleaned and mothproofed by cleaning experts. Do not become an instant expert and use mothproofing spray directly on garments—this will cause discoloration. Store only in closets where some air can circulate. If suede is worth having, it's worth taking care of.

Jeans

America's trendiest fashion originated in France 500 years ago

—and still going strong

Everyone has owned a pair of jeans. Worn them out, turned them into cut-offs, and finally thrown them away. Every time someone looks at you in your jeans they make decisions about you, so maybe it's time you thought about which type and design is right for you.

American jean manufacturers produce millions of pairs of jeans each year; the jean and the family of apparel related to it reflect a popularity unique and unmatched in the history of fashion.

The amount of denim, corduroy, and other fabrics now used in the manufacturing of jeans and jeanswear is enough to circle the planet Earth 22 times at the equator and still have more than a couple of yards to spare.

Jeans were first written about in 1567, according to the

Shorter Oxford English dictionary, and the fabric is said to have originated in the 500-year-old textile center of Nimes, France. It was called denim from the contraction "from Nimes" or "de Nimes."

For us in America, however, denim really came alive when the American western blue denim jean was created in the mid-1800s to provide economical pants suitable for the hard work of shaping a growing nation. After World War II, the baby boom of the '40s and '50s created a new young population group that grew up in jeans and adopted them as a symbol—the blue denim society of the '60s.

Then in the '70s, the blue denim looks were embraced by the fashion world; now they are seen everywhere. Jeans and their manufacturers have made us very label conscious. Whether it is a name brand from the major producers, private labels from major chains, or designer logos, jeans have become a major presence in the world of fashion and work wear. They are seen everywhere: shopping, sightseeing, at sports events, even in the evenings. You'll find them in palaces and in the White House, on rock stars and construction workers. "People" magazine's fifth anniversary issue readers' poll reported jeans and jogging shoes as THE clothes everybody loved. They've become a kind of security blanket.

They're not all bad, you know. If bought correctly, jeans are a great money-saver and rarely wear out or go out of style. They certainly have a high recognition factor.

Exactly what are jeans? Two yards of denim go into the typical pair of jeans. They often have a flat-fell seam and panel stitching sometimes called track-stitching; sometimes this is done in contrasting white or colored thread. This double seam adds strength, securely holding the back and front of the garment together. The double needle seam is different from that on regular trousers, which have pressed open seams.

Jeans have a self waistband or no waistband; some come with self belt lops, yoke back, patch hip pockets and two patch back pockets. Those back pockets are often the billboards for a label or stitched logo or design.

The classic jean has five pockets. The more traditional style you buy, the longer they will stay in style.

Remember—your build and your age determine what kind you wear. Avoid a skin-tight fit, flashy detailing, and extreme cuts and fabrics. You can only look bad in them if you wear the wrong kind! Wear them tight enough to display your physical attributes, loose enough to let them know you are a gentleman.

Selecting Glasses and Sunglasses

Wear your glasses and sunglasses as you do with your clothes. You can look scholarly, businesslike or pure pleasure— it all depends on the frames and your face.

The proper eye glass frames can bring strength and authority to a man's appearance.

They provide telltale clues to who you are. The dark horn-rims are the basic business frame. Steel or gold frames give a more sophisticated look. And if you need glasses for close work or for reading, the half-rim or half-moon shapes are the best. They can be slipped into your top handkerchief pocket where they take up little space. I have also noticed the growing trend among men to wear contact lenses. This of course is a personal choice.

The smart executive wears his glasses or his contacts as he does his clothing—to accomplish the task at hand. You should buy your eye glass frames to bring confidence to your clients— not compliments from them.

Here are some tips on buying frames. Take along a friend,

whose judgment you trust. Remember, this isn't an ego trip, this is business. If that can't be worked out, select three good quality frames. Then, in the quiet of your home, try them on and make a deliberated decision with no one pushing you into what they like.

• First, have patience. Try on many frames—50 or 75 if need be—to find the one pair you will be happy with in terms of comfort and a businesslike authoritative appearance.

• The pupils of your eye should be centered within the frames when you look into a mirror.

• The color of the frames should coordinate well with your coloring.

• As a general rule, buy a frame shape which is opposite to the shape of your face. If you have the perfect oval shape, you can wear anything. Keep trying on frames until you find a pair that feels comfortable and looks good.

• A round face will seem slimmer with square frames. A square face will seem fuller with a round shape. The oblong face needs width, so try glasses that extend beyond the side of your face.

Choosing the tint for your sunglasses is really the same as above. Opticians, however, all claim that gray offers the most protection for the eyes. Green, brown and gold are the next best. Blue, pink and yellow shades do not really give much protection for your eyes.

Take care of your glasses. Don't take glasses off with only one hand. Don't let the lenses get scratched when setting them on a surface. Try to purchase the new plastic lenses; they scratch far less than glass if you moisten them before cleaning.

If you seem to be pushing your glasses back onto your nose, check with an optician or eye center to see if your frames need tightening or adjusting.

We are faced with choosing from hundreds of sunglass styles, a multitude of lens types or colors, and a broad range in prices. Just remember: Don't hurry. Your eyes are the focus of your face. Give them the attention they deserve.

Luggage is Part of Your Wardrobe

Luggage should be an extension of your wardrobe, an accessory that transmits to those you meet instant information about your income, background and position in the business world. Living in a mobile society as we do, we can no longer be content with luggage that is found on a sale table or hand-me-downs from friends and relatives.

In the old days, suitcases (as they were called) fell into two class distinctions. Gentlemen owned leather suitcases, usually carried about by porters. For long trips that required large amounts of clothing, there were steamer trunks which traveled aboard ships and on long distance train journeys.

Today, there is a wide assortment of luggage to fit anyone's budget. And this luggage is lighter, stronger and more versatile than ever before. It is constructed not only to maximize packaging space, but also to provide ease of transportation.

When you buy luggage, think in terms of a once-in-a-lifetime purchase and buy the best quality you can afford.

There are basically three types of luggage. First is what we call hard luggage, generally characterized by the solid form or rigid sides. If you decide on hard luggage, stay away from the obvious plastic ones. Stay with a good vinyl or Naugahyde that looks like leather, or if possible purchase the real thing—leather.

The second type is soft-walled luggage, a relative newcomer. It has the great advantage of allowing the traveler to overstuff if need be. The soft walls are shaped by laminated wood or metal, and the sides are usually canvas, vinyl or leather, which allows that extra stretch. The other big plus for this type of luggage is its lighter weight.

For short trips, the carry-on has made the size 22 by 13 by 7 inches a new magic number. It allows you to beat the crowd to the taxi stand and get away from the airport quickly. This size comes in both hard and soft luggage.

A new dimension in transporting clothes is the garment bag, which comes in cloth, vinyl, plastic, leather and canvas. This, too, can be carried on planes and thrown in the back of the car or hung up during the flight or drive. A lot of clothes can be carried on and off a plane or in a car in a garment bag and carry-on.

When choosing your luggage, always choose a style that represents you and your family. If it looks right for business, it will always work for pleasure. But the reverse is not true.

When you are ready to purchase your luggage, take your time. Remember, it is going to last you a long time. Do some comparative shopping in department stores and luggage specialty stores. Here are some tips to remember when shopping:

• Buy all your luggage in the same material and color, including your garment bag and carry-on.

• Check the handles and their reinforcement. Think of the bags as full and heavy. Are the handles comfortable? Do they seem strong enough?

• Does the garment bag zipper slide easily? Fold easily? Does it have a good, strong handle? Extra pockets? Is it easy to handle?

• If you're buying canvas luggage, are there any loose ends in the fabric? If so, it will unravel and come apart at the seams.

• Make sure there are generous seam allowances (amount of fabric on each side of the seam) so they won't pull away.

- Remember, the thicker the material, the tougher it is and the longer it will wear. If it is thin nylon, check for strength and check the stitching.
- The more stitching on a fabric bag, the stronger the reinforcement. Two or three rows of stitching are better than one.
- Any belts or weight-bearing reinforcements should be as large as possible.
- When the stitching starts to pull away, get it fixed. If it is not covered under the original warranty, you can probably have it repaired at your shoe repair shop.

Question and Answer Time

Readers frequently ask questions about how a particular fashion originated. I have put together a list of "where did it come from."

Q. Where did the name "blazer" come from?

A. It is said that it started aboard H.M.S. Blazer. The captain of the English ship, looking over his motley crew, decided to spruce them up. So he gave them all metal-buttoned blue serge jackets to wear. From then on, this jacket was called the "blazer."

Q. Where did we get the cutaway coat?

A. The original cutaway coat was the riding coat for early country gentlemen. They had the front cut away to free the knees when riding. They used the buttons on the back for looping the tails so that they wouldn't get in the way when astride a horse.

Q. How did trouser cuffs come into use?

A. Men used to have straps attached to the bottom of their

trousers of their military uniforms to keep them down. After the straps disappeared, plain-bottom trousers came into fashion. Later, when men would walk through open country, they started turning up the bottoms of their trousers to avoid the underbrush.

Q. The Chesterfield coat has a velvet collar. Why?

A. The velvet on the collar of the Chesterfield first came into being as a sign of disapproval of the many executions during the French Revolution. Even the men of other countries added the velvet collars to their coats as a mark of mourning and disapproval. Since then it has become a mark of fashion.

Q. Did we always have lapels on coats? From where did they come?

A. Lapels on the jacket came into being from early military uniforms. Soldiers, wanting to be comfortable, unfastened the upper button on the high collared tunics and rolled back each side. The custom gradually caught on in civilian clothes.

Q. Where did the four-in-hand tie knot come from?

A. That goes way back to old England when the men who rode on top of the coach and four were among the first to wear the tie knotted, hence came the name "four-in-hand."

Q. Why are there buttons on the cuffs of men's jackets?

A. Today there is no use for the buttons on the sleeve, but when they were first sewn on, they served a definite purpose. Buttons were a simple means for holding the sleeve from hanging down and impeding movement.

In the 17th century, men spent a lot of money on their clothes and especially in the jackets, so they tried to avoid anything that would soil or damage them. To keep cuffs out of harm's way, they were turned back, and so they would not fall down, they were buttoned. Also, if it was cold or windy, the wide sleeve could be tightened or closed around the wrist.

In centuries past this was also a prevalent way to show wealth. A man often displayed it by adorning his jacket sleeve.

The buttons on military uniforms are said to have started for a totally different reason. Some say it was Napoleon, some say it was a king's displeasure when he saw some of his men wiping their noses on their sleeves. To make this impossible, buttons were required on all sleeves.

Q. Each time I sit down I grab my pants and pull them up so I won't stretch them, yet I find that after a while, when I hold my pants up or stand straight, I can see that the knees still bag a little. Is there anything I can do about this?

A. Yes. For any pants that are of a soft material such as cashmere, flannel or tweed, have your tailor put in what they call a "silk knee." It should be fitted eight inches above and eight inches below the center of the knee. This lets the material slip easily over the knee and not stretch as much. Also, when you sit down, reach down and take with the thumb and fore finger the crease of the pants, pulling it up and then moving the crease inside the knees. Do not just pull your pants up. Pull up and then move the crease to the inside of your pants legs.

One of the interesting questions I keep getting from my readers is: Do you or don't you button that last button on your vest?

I am sure you have heard the story of Beau Brummel and his pal, Louis XVI. In his time Beau Brummel was the last word in sartorial attire on the Continent. His word was undisputed when it came to any clothing question.

At one of the big parties Louis came in and all the men were laughing behind his back, as it seemed he forgot to button his bottom vest button.

Since Louis was, for lack of a better word, fat, it was a logical omission because he could not see over his tummy.

Well, of course, Beau Brummel came to his pal's rescue and announced that a gentleman always leaves the bottom button unbuttoned.

Fashion was created instantly. And from that time on, gentlemen always left the last button on their vests unbuttoned.

But life today is not that simple.

As the years passed we moved into a business environment where sloppiness or an undisciplined look spark negative remarks.

If the vest is cut on a straight line of buttons, then you should button the last one. If you don't, it looks as if you forgot.

Many suits today are cut and tailored so that the last button on the vest is on the bias.

This means there are at least six buttons on the vest and the last one is put at the bottom where the vest starts to spread.

If a gentleman decided to button that last button it would make the vest puckered, as it was cut not to be buttoned at the bottom, carrying out the Beau Brummel tradition.

So here we have a choice of judgment. What you have been led to believe by tradition today may not always hold true.

As both kinds of vests are made today by the finest of

designers and manufacturers, you become once more your own arbiter of fashion.

Babies haven't any hair;
Old man's heads are just as bare;
Between the cradle and the grave
Lies a haircut and a shave.
—Samuel Hoffenstein, 1890- 1947

16

HAIR, BEARDS AND MUSTACHES

Norman H. Anderson and his associates in a very interesting study obtained the likableness ratings of five hundred and fifty-five different words that are used as personality trait descriptions. Subjects rated each word on a seven point scale ranging from least favorable or desirable to most favorable or desirable. The averaging ratings given each word by one hundred college students give us the value for that word. This value gives us an indication of different traits which influence the judgment people make of others as based on appearance. The ranking of these traits is very interesting through what it reveals about our preferences in general. "Sincere" was rated most favorable of all five hundred and fifty-five terms, while "liar" and "phony" are the very least desirable. The ten most favorable ratings are given below:

1. Sincere

2. Honest
3. Understanding
4. Loyal
5. Truthful
6. Trustworthy
7. Intelligent
8. Dependable
9. Open-minded
10. Thoughtful

Hair, beards and mustaches must show you as sincere, honest, truthful, trustworthy and dependable. For example, the cut and arrangement of the hair has been one of the most basic status representations among all cultures of the world. Therefore, the trimming and arrangement of your hair must be consistent and designed to suggest these five highly rated traits to the people you meet. Inconsistency in appearance creates instant suspicion in the minds of those we meet, therefore we must take care that our hair style and facial hair are consistent with the rest of the look we present. A classic suit and tie, white shirt, and conservative shoes, topped off by a long-haired, bearded image would create instant suspicion in anyone's mind and you set up a conflict in the unconscious mind.

Lengths of Hair

The length of a man's hair is a very personal statement of how he sees himself. Your hair is your crown ego; unfortunately, no one else sees you quite like you see yourself. Since people make superficial judgments about you based on the length of your hair, your should be aware of how others relate to it. You must then decide what it is you want your hair to say about you. Let's briefly analyze how people react to different lengths of hair.

Long hair—To most people, long hair connotes the artistic, aesthetic, romantic, and casual mode of life. Discipline, seriousness, and business ethics are not suggested by long hair.

Moderate Length—A moderate length of hair, however, suggests pragmatic, executive, businesslike, serious, and decisive qualities. This cut suggests a straightforward reasonableness that is acceptable to everyone.

Very Short or Brush—The keywords here are energetic, precise, athletic, and youthful. A word of caution is necessary. Extremely short hair has some negative connotations. It suggest an inability to conform to the obligations of adult life. This style implies the perennial freshman who is stubborn and unreasonable.

Since I am addressing this book to the individual who desires to succeed, a moderate hair length is recommended. This length of hair is received well by anyone you are likely to meet in most business situations. Unless you are a rock star or the like, the most practical guide is to be sure that your hair length does not detract from what you are about to say. You can hardly communicate with someone if he is busy wondering about the length of your hair, who did your curls, or how your Afro feels to the touch.

A few simple rules. Keep your hair length moderate. Keep it clean. Keep it neat. Keep it simple. If everyone is telling you or thinking how great your hair looks, they are not listening to what you have to say. Instead, they are probably wondering how you have time for anything but taking care of your hair. Even in Hollywood, the people who handle the rock star's money certainly don't look like rock stars. They look like businessmen.

Styling

The men's fashion world has devoted a great deal of attention recently to the subject of having one's hair styled to conform to your facial configuration, correct or improve imperfections, or highlight good facial features. In theory, such an approach to hair styling can be helpful and rewarding. In practice, however, frequently all you do is trade one distraction for another, or create a distraction where there was none in the first place. Remember, the imperfections we were all given are natural and honest. People understand them and feel secure with them. Artificial attempts to cover them up only make people more aware of them. For example, styling your hair in an excessive length to frame an oval face only creates the problem of long hair. The key here is moderation. There are many excellent hair stylists today who understand the concepts involved. You must simply keep their enthusiasm in check. Your hair style shouldn't be a masterpiece or a work of art, but a simple undistracting complement to your face.

A few simple rules. The hair on the back of the neck should be tapered to its natural length, not a swing or block cut. Frequent trims are much better than infrequent overhauls, since the best hair style is the one which neither looks like it needs attention nor has just had it. Stick with one style. The man whose hair style is always the same never seems to age, even in photographs—an interesting and important fact for everyone, not just the business executive. The young man of today should have hair styled so that if his children were to look at his wedding pictures twenty years from now, he wouldn't have to make any explanations. The style should be classic, and remain so.

Finding a Hair Stylist or Barber

The most important criterion to use in finding a hair stylist or barber is that he follow *your* instructions, not *his* creative urge or latest whim. You must feel comfortable in his shop and have confidence in him. Your stylist or barber should take the pattern of your head and cut your hair with an eye toward proper balance. Price is never a criterion, but confidence always is.

Sideburns

A man's sideburns should be tapered and lend balance to the shape of his head. The length of the sideburns should not extend past the center of the ear. The sideburns should be straight and not trimmed in the western style. The western style and exaggerated bushy sideburns give a man a very rural and unsophisticated look, which is not recommended for serious business. When shaving with a razor, be sure to wipe off the lather from the sideburn before you trim it so you can compare the length of both sideburns. You then avoid an unbalanced look caused by sideburns being unequal in length. You can also easily trim the sideburn straight across, rather than have it canted in either direction. Properly trimmed sideburns in the correct length give a man a knowledgeable, sophisticated, and dependable air.

The Part

Very few men can wear their hair without using a part. For those who can, simplicity should be highlighted. Avoid any exaggerated "Valentino" look. For the rest of us, we must give careful attention to finding the correct part line. Your line should be parted at the peak recession point of the hair line. This natural parting line conveys an erudite, refined, and reasonable image. Don't make the mistake of trying to part your hair to hide the recession line. This simply draws attention to it.

Shampooing

Clean, healthy looking hair is an asset in every aspect of life. With the high pollution counts in our air today, keeping your hair clean and healthy looking requires some effort on your part. Since very few people wear hats now, the natural oils in your hair readily pick up the contaminants in the air and give your hair a dull, dirty look. You must work out a routine that works for you. Ask your hair stylist to recommend a few shampoos that are designed for your type of hair—oily, regular, or dry. Experiment with them but shampoo a maximum of twice a week. You can keep your hair clean by rinsing it well each day in the shower without damaging it through shampooing too often. If you have thick hair, give it two washings rather than one big soaping up then rinse it clean. Be easy on your hair, don't rub-dry too hard but let it dry naturally or use a hand dryer. I have found that by rinsing my hair every morning in the shower, I never have dandruff. Clean, healthy looking, well-groomed hair suggests responsibility. Dirty, dull, unkempt hair conveys disorganization and unreliableness.

Hair Control

Again, experiment with oils, creams, or preparations until you find one that will control your hair but leave it looking natural. Be sure you find one which can easily be rinsed out. Try to avoid sprays because their alcohol content makes your hair brittle and easily split. Aim for the natural look, neither dried-out nor oily and slick. Keep some of the preparation that works for you at the office so you can freshen up during the day or between calls.

Hair Coloring

There are two looks which you must avoid at all costs. One is the jet-black dye job which makes your face chalky white. The other is long gray hair worn over the ears, making you look like an old, old, hippie. Try to achieve a happy medium by using enough coloring to give your hair a natural, youthful look. The blending of some gray in a man's hair gives him character, depth, and a look of wisdom. It matches the complexion better and suggests maturity.

Baldness

The most handsome man I ever chummed around with was bald. He packaged himself and presented himself so well that his lack of hair was the least important thing about him. I always had the feeling that if he had not been bald, he would have shaved the center part of his head anyway. Wearing a hairpiece is a personal decision. However, again you must avoid extremes. Don't wear a hairpiece or wig which is unnatural or exaggerated and attracts attention to itself. If you are partially bald, keep what hair you have neatly trimmed for a natural look.

There is one big mistake you must avoid. Don't try combing your hair differently to hide a bald spot. Lowering your part, slicking your hair over or brushing it up to cover a bald spot only attracts attention to the problem. You magnify the problem and people look at your hair to see what you're trying to hide and this weakens your position. The partially bald individual, with closely trimmed remaining hair, presents a strong, dependable, and confident image.

Beards

Beards are like sunglasses. As long as they are on your face, no one will really get to know you or trust you. Creative people, artists, art directors, and writers are the exceptions who may wear beards. Their background, education, trustworthiness and future is of no importance to you when you evaluate their work. Only the picture, poem, or book handed to you at that moment counts. Their work stands on its own merit and the value is in the eye of the beholder.

For those of us who must sell ourselves to the people we meet every day, a beard is not recommended. You shouldn't be misled into wearing a beard to correct another problem. For example, wearing a beard to hide a double chin is not the answer. Look at the rest of you. You're probably overweight and the double chin is the symptom—not the problem. If you feel you must wear a beard, then wear a neatly trimmed moderate length beard shaped by a barber into a classic style. Nothing destroys credibility and confidence faster than a scraggly, unkempt or exaggerated beard.

Mustaches

Mustaches have been an on-again off-again phenomenon throughout the history of our country. Since our country is presently youth oriented, the mustache, which connotes maturity, is considered an affectation to many. If you must wear a mustache, and some men do successfully, make sure it is neatly trimmed and clean. The pencil thin or waxed-end mustache is to be avoided at all costs since it makes you a caricature. A natural, well-trimmed mustache can be worn, but only at your own risk. It must never curve around your mouth or come below your upper lip. The carpet-bagger style, made famous by Victor Jory in *Gone With the Wind* or the Fu Manchu mustache, always synonymous with evil, certainly makes dealing with people an uphill struggle.

In summary, every study I've been able to find indicates that people over forty in American society don't trust a man whose hair covers his ears or drops below the upper edge of his collar. Since we have seen how important the traits of sincerity, trustworthiness, honesty, truthfulness, and dependability are in the rankings of personality traits, it is not hard to see that long hair or unkempt facial hair is not part of the impression or image we want to present to those who are important in our lives. Remember, moderation is the key. Package yourself and your appearance to convey those important traits to the people you meet, particularly watching your hair style. Since American business is controlled by people over forty, it's safe to say that long hair is not an asset to the man who would move up.

17

TO SOAP OR NOT TO SOAP

The cornerstone of any personal packaging program begins with cleanliness. Personal hygiene is the foundation upon which you can begin to plan the image you want to present to the world. A clean, scrubbed look conveys that you are alert, energetic, and well-organized. In addition, a clean, well-groomed appearance indicates to others that you respect yourself; consequently, they too can respect you.

I like to call the mechanics of grooming, Personal Assertiveness Training. As I mentioned earlier, our self-concept of ourselves is enhanced by the favorable responses from those we hold important. Therefore, by carefully grooming myself, I know that I will present a good image to those I meet. In addition, I also know that everyone reacts favorably to a clean, well-groomed appearance. As I prepare myself for the day through proper grooming, I equip myself with the self-confidence and self-respect to conduct my affairs with a sure and steady hand, no matter what trials lay ahead. I know I'll look clean and well-groomed, and I know everyone reacts favorably to this. Consequently, I develop a confidence and liking for myself. For this reason, I approach the very act of grooming like a personal and very easy sort of assertiveness training. Look good on the outside, feel good on the inside. Try it yourself.

If I had my way we would find out who invented soap and erect a statue in his or her honor. Soap, my friend, is the cornerstone of packaging—social, business, and personal. There is no such thing as being dressed right and being badly groomed. I am dedicating this chapter to all the beautiful and adorable women who are graciously and patiently overlooking some bad personal habits of the men in their lives. Of course, reading this chapter doesn't mean I'm talking about you, right?

There are three things that make a man or woman attractive and desirable as the years go on—cleanliness, slimness, and wardrobe. The latter I've written a book about, so let's get back to the first of these, and make no mistake, pal, I am talking to you.

Now don't go back to your wife or girl friend and say,"Honey, do I smell okay?" She is going to look at you and say, "Honey, you are Mr. Clean himself." Then she will smile her way out of the room, all the while asking for forgiveness from above her for what she has just said. Frankly, I am appalled at the way men (on the average) take care of themselves. So, it is shocking when I meet someone scrubbed-looking, with his hair combed neatly. I want to race over to him and say, "Pal, are you married? If not, I know a dozen women who would like to meet a scrubbed-looking guy for a change." They don't care if you have a job or not, because you can get one if you want one. People identify with cleanliness. If a man has a scrubbed look, then his mind, his habits, and his work must be similar. It gets to the point where I resent some men because they smell bad or look like they smell lousy. I don't want to go on and on, but I do want to communicate that this is a vital part of looking right. Every morning you take a shower or bath. I know almost everyone showers nowadays, but I'm taking no chances. After your shower or bath, dry off and start getting your act together. Comb your hair (refer to the chapter on hair grooming for information, cut, etc.). You may think that advising you to comb your hair is oversimplifying, but I can assure you that, for some, the idea is novel. When shaving, check all facial hair. If you're over thirty, invest in a good pair of tweezers to pick out wandering hairs on your nose and cheeks. Also, invest in a good magnifying mirror. Once each week closely examine your face. When you buy tweezers pick up a small pair of scissors to trim nasal hair too. There is a special type of scissors made for this trimming.

Now you look in the mirror to be sure everything looks good. Brush your teeth and, again, if you are over thirty, use a mouthwash. Try them all and see which one works best for you. Frankly, gentlemen, they are all the same. Just find one you like. Use a mouthwash to start every day and any time you'll be near your wife or lover. It not only refreshes your mouth and breath, it's a morale booster, too. Keep one at the office.

If your teeth yellow easily, you can clean them better with a mixture of salt and baking soda. Follow that with full-strength hydrogen peroxide. Swish it around in your mouth until it foams well, then hold it there for at least a minute. Rinse with water and do your regular brushing. Within a year your teeth will be whiter than they've ever been. Keep a toothbrush at the office and use it.

There are two schools of thought on underarm care. First, there are men who are ardent lovers of the great Tarzan movies and let nature have its way. They must remember that Tarzan was the only good guy in Africa at that time. Remember, the "Big Jock" is only exciting to watch from the bleachers, not when you encounter him in the sweaty locker room. Then there is the second group, absolutely right, who hold that you must use some kind of underarm deodorant. Don't dump it on anytime and think you are going to cover up the odor. Shower. Use a roll-on, a push-up, a spray-on, but use something!

Now, look in the mirror. You are "Mr. Clean." Your skin has that beautiful glow of cleanliness. Your mouth feels clean and your hair is in place. Your hope you bump into someone, because you smell delicious.

Now, we quickly check the extremities, toenails and fingernails. I have seen great-looking guys and for some unknown reason looked at their feet and have gotten weird feelings that there must be something wrong inside them to let their toenails grow out that way. Dirty, gray-brown nails have the appearance of a man with a psychological problem. Buy one large toenail clipper and use it. Every ten days or two weeks check your toe nails. Cut them straight across. Do not cut them around the corners, that is how ingrown toenails start.

Check your fingernails. There are several theories on this. One is to use a file to clean under the nails. I find using a little stiff bristled fingernail brush keeps my nails not only immaculately clean, but it softens my cuticles so that at my leisure I can push them back after a good scrubbing. This gives your hands a genteel look. Trim your nails so they are always short and rounded. Have a manicure if you can. But please just get them buffed, no polish. If you like the buffed look, and can't afford or do not want to spend the money, pick up a buffer and some buffing cream and do your own nails whenever you feel they need it. You can keep them looking great for practically nothing.

Make no mistake, cleanliness is the foundation where all personal packaging starts and is a beautiful way to project respect and regard for your own body. We relate cleanliness to energy, and if there is one thing the world does not need it is more tired blood.

Divide your day into three parts. Shower and get your act together every morning. Then wash your face and hands and comb your hair, once between breakfast and lunch, obviously right after lunch, and once between lunch and the end of the working day. So whenever you see anyone, you'll have that clean, neat look and they will subconsciously recognize this must be the way you run all your affairs.

I hired a beautiful typist to get this book in order to send to my publisher. Her one salient remark was, "For my money you could have written a book, instead of a chapter, on cleanliness for men."

Re-read this chapter. Do it for yourself, for your loved ones, or for a close friend and for your future. Perhaps the best way to sum up the importance of cleanliness is to relate it to an indefinable look which some people seem to possess—class. Think of the people in your life whom you automatically label class. As you picture them in your mind, consider the fact that those who have that class look invariably have cleanliness as an unmistakable part of their image. Although you've probably never analyzed it, you should now visualize them without that clean, well-groomed look, you certainly could not think of them as possessing class. Remember, assert yourself. Develop your self-confidence by knowing your clean, well-groomed appearance will be favorably judged by anyone you meet.

Taking Proper Care of the Scalp Can Preserve the Hair

Do you get a sinking feeling in the morning when you see all that hair in the bathtub or bathroom sink? Relax. It isn't as serious as it looks.

Your hair falls out and grows back in continuously at an average growth of three to five years. At the end of the cycle, each hair detaches itself from its papilla and moves the follicle until it falls out, while the papilla remains at rest for awhile and then starts synthesizing materials for a new hair. Most men have about 12 square inches of scalp and about 1,090 hairs to each square inch, which amounts to approximately 12,000 hairs. So don't worry about the hair you lose. Follow a good grooming routine to keep it healthy and it will keep replacing itself.

The first rule in keeping your hair and scalp healthy and vigorous is to be always on the alert for any possible scalp disorder. Keep an eye open for symptoms like itchy or inflamed scalp, uncontrollable dandruff, scaling or increased oiliness. In their early stages, such problems can usually be brought under control very easily. In a stubborn or complicated case, it is advisable to consult an expert.

Many people view dandruff as just an inevitable fact of life. This is a mistake. If you take steps at the first signs of dandruff, you often can bring it under control before it goes out of hand. A scalp normally sheds dead cells regularly and unnoticeably as a form of self-renewal. This sloughing process becomes dandruff when the cycle speeds up abnormally and dead skin tissues appear on your shoulders. Alcohol and spicy food contribute to dandruff, and whatever increases blood circulation and stimulates the oil glands can aggravate the condition.

Once dandruff is gone and hair and scalp are back to normal, it is time to think of the right conditioner to give your hair the control and body it needs. Hair has a certain porousness that allows conditioners to penetrate and give it body and manageability which make it easier to comb and control. There are liquid conditioners for every type of hair texture and degree of oiliness. They are usually applied after a shampoo, then rinsed out, but always find out what the label recommends. One conditioning treatment usually lasts through several shampoos.

There are also shampoos with built in conditioners. Choose them according to the condition you are trying to correct. If you have coarse hair that is difficult to comb, use a regular cream rinse to soften it and make it tangle free. Fine hair will benefit from a rinse conditioner with extra protein content for extra body. This type of shampoo is also recommended for adding volume to thin hair. The label on the bottle will alert you to it.

Blow drying is the No. 1 culprit when it comes to hair damage, but blow drying need not be harmful if done properly. The most damaging time to blow dry hair is in the last few minutes of drying when hair goes from damp to dry. To cut down on the damage, use the hot setting at the start, holding the dryer at arms length away from your hair until it is merely damp. Then switch to warm or cool and hold it closer to finish drying and styling.

If your hair has been damaged, use a reconditioning rinse. If heavily damaged, give your hair a deep conditioning treatment every few weeks. Of course you may feel that it needs a rinse every day and a shampoo only once a week. Adjust your hair care to your own particular needs.

A comb can also damage your hair. Mass produced plastic combs are poured into fast extrusion molds, popped out and sold by the millions without quality control or the filing away of rough spots. Some of those combs have teeth with razor sharp edges that will shred your hair as you comb. Others may have only one or two defective teeth, but will inflict damage over a period of time. When you run a defective comb through your hair and feel it pull and tug, don't persist: Throw it away.

When buying a new comb, run your thumbnail between its teeth and check for sharpness and rough spots on which your nail snags. The comb you buy should have smooth, rounded teeth and not too close together on the side. There are good combs on the market and price is not always an index of quality.

The Skin You Love to Touch?

Let's talk about skin. No matter where you are or what your objectives, it is important that your skin looks good.

If you view your skin under a microscope, you would see millions of tiny skin cells struggling for life. There is a continuous flow of blood, nourishing a production line that seems unending. As the blood feeds each cell, the newer ones underneath drive the older cells to the surface of the skin where they lose form and eventually scale off.

There are two basic types of glands: sweat and oil. The sweat glands cover practically all parts of the body, helping to eliminate poisons. The oil glands consist of little sacs of oil that lubricate.

If the oil glands are under-active because of poor health, age or weather, then the oil does not flow freely and there is a loss of tone and elasticity in the skin and this leaves healthy skin full of lines and wrinkles.

From birth to teens, the skin is usually normal in tone, texture and appearance. It's during the teen years when all the changes occur in the glandular activity. At young adulthood, your skin should return to normal — not too dry and not too oily.

For those in middle age and beyond, your skin has a tendency to dehydrate, to lose its tension and elasticity, making wrinkles and lines deeper.

How can we slow down the process of aging? Here are some very basic rules to keep in mind:

Since your skin is the point of entry for bacteria, the use of soap and water is by far the most important and beneficial way of removing the contaminants.

Normal skin reacts best to transparent, glycerine soap, because its retention of water is greater. It is low in alkali content and maintains the normal acid mantle of the skin.

For oily skin, a pure bland soap removes all oil from oily skin without irritation.

For dry and extra dry skin, use the super fatted soaps that contain fats and oils that help lubricate fine, sensitive dry skin. If you have blemished skin, follow the advice of a dermatologist and get a medicated soap or lotion for any problems causing heavy oil or acne skin conditions. You will find a germicidal skin lotion (sometimes prescribed by a dermatologist) is non-irritating, non-alkaline, hypo-allergenic and more effective than soap.

It is also important for a man to wash his hands and face and comb his hair several times a day. At home always use a wash cloth to keep away blackheads and whiteheads, paying special attention to the ears, temples, the sides of your nose and hard-to-get places where blackheads start.

Never use extremely hot or extremely cold water, as either one may shock the skin and cause broken blood vessels.

Shaving Can Become a Real Pick-Me-Up

If you are reading this book you are familiar with a golden rule of life. If a man can't find time to take care of himself, he can't find time to take care of my business.

We shave every morning. Many men have to shave again if they are going to an important function in the evening. Shaving is a normal routine event in every man's day; but let's intellectualize this a bit and turn a functional routine into an event to be looked forward to instead of dreaded each morning.

We all know that not all beards are created equal. They classified beards into three types: normal, sensitive and heavy. These alternatives create an interesting and helpful break-through for men, because a shave can become a real pick-up each morning. We can give ourselves a cosmetic lift and improve our appearance in such a way that we see and feel the results immediately.

Women have always been much more secure in the use of cosmetics; we macho men, until lately, have denied ourselves the right to self-indulge. Psychologically, the effect of having a great feeling around our face and head can give us a superstart on a busy day.

Even the men who use an electric razor should, at least once a week, use soap and a razor to (1) trim the sideburns and give them a crisp, clean line; and (2) shave off any difficult-to- reach or fine hair from the face or neck.

If you show up at work with a bad shave, you have already got two strikes on you. Here are a few tips for getting a clean, well-groomed shave:

(1) Hold the razor under very warm running water (water that's too hot will warp blades, resulting in razor pull and irritation). Never apply a cool blade to your face (too abrasive).

(2) Apply shaving product as evenly as possible. If applied too thickly, it clogs the blade and reduces performance; too thinly, your skin forfeits necessary protection.

(3) Leave shave product on your face for at least 30 seconds to one minute to really soften the beard.

(4) Shave sides of face first in the direction beard grows. (To determine direction: Run hand over beard before shaving. If it scratches, you're going against the grain.)

(5) Shave upper lip and chin next. These areas have denser growth and coarser bristle and require more softening time.

(6) Shave neck area last (a delicate spot, so be careful). The best method is to shave up from the base of the throat, and then from the chin down to the base of the throat (beard grows in both directions).

(7) Rinse face with warm water, then cool. Towel dry.

Extra shaving tips:

—For the closest shave of all, shave twice: first with the grain, re-lather lightly, and then shave against the grain.

—Don't press razor too firmly against face. Use one long, smooth stroke instead of short, quick uneven ones.

—Don't keep blades for more than two weeks. As soon as you feel the razor pull even slightly, it's time to change blades. Dull blades cause razor rash and irritation.

—Always use two hands when shaving. One hand pulls the skin up taut, while the other guides the blade.

This is the Law of the Yukon, that only the strong shall thrive; That surely the weak shall perish, and only the fit survive.

—Robert William Service

18

FITNESS FOR FITTING

While you develop your packaging program, let's not forget the product itself—your body. To be successful, you must keep your physical equipment in sound, running order. In addition, keeping fit gives a healthy, toned look which is attractive and friendly. This healthy, fit look gives people confidence in you, as well as providing more assertiveness training. By keeping fit, you not only look good, you physically feel good, and emotionally like yourself better. On the other hand, an overweight or flabby appearance suggests some very negative connotations to those you meet. If you are not disciplined enough to control your weight, how can you possibly be disciplined enough to handle someone's affairs or money.

Exercise is like sex, it's nonaccumulative and must be repeated often to enjoy the benefits. What makes life interesting is that you can always improve yourself in any area— all you need is interest. I don't want to take up too much space in a book on clothing, but we are talking about the frame we are hanging the clothes on. The firmer and thinner the frame the more elegant and desirable the look. Need I say more?

There are really only two basic exercises that are endorsed and encouraged by the medical profession—jogging and swimming. Of course, if you are not by water or have your own pool, you concentrate on jogging. By all means get a medical examination. Swimming and jogging are the easiest and cheapest of all exercises. All you need to swim or jog is a swim suit or a good pair of running shoes. Both are great cardiovascular exercises. The heart pushes fresh blood completely through the body every fifteen minutes of jogging or swimming. Everywhere new blood is pumped, new cells are growing giving new life and new energy. These exercises are programmed to balance the body. They reduce the hips, thighs, and waist at the same time, not building up anywhere else. The only other physical change is that the stomach is flattened and tightened up. It is so simple. Feel better, look better.

Swimming, like jogging, seems to be the great activator allowing the blood to surge to all parts of the body giving life and vitality. Show me a man or woman who extends himself or herself in exercises and you will find an attractive person. One of the most handsome men I knew was Buster Crabb, the great Tarzan and olympic swimmer. Buster and I worked on *Kraft Theatre*. One day I told him how great he looked. He floored me when he told me the number of pool lengths he swam every morning for his exercise. You should do it just for the skin tone alone. Those who are disciplined will reap the benefits all their lives. The great faces in Hollywood look that way because they are disciplined. Their look is their product. Before and during every picture each star has a training program tailored to keep that lean, hard, masculine look, the one you thought they were just born with and didn't earn or work to keep. During a picture many stars work out before each scene just to keep that gaunt look he was famous for. People relate thinness to energy, preciseness, health, and alertness. They attribute these same qualities to the thin person's business and private life. Everything I've said here about men goes for women too, make no mistake about it.

Driving out Sunset Boulevard to the ocean one Sunday, I realized I was passing Jayne Mansfield's home. One could hardly miss it. She had bought Rudy Vallee's old estate, and had the house and surrounding walls done all in pink. (I mean pink!). Pulling in, I found the gates closed, so I walked to the entrance and pressed the intercom button. Soon I heard, "Yes, who is it?" Well, I played Jayne's husband on Broadway in *Will Success Spoil Rock Hunter* for two and one-half years, so I just yelled, "It's Bronk Baby," one of our old lines in the show. She laughed and said, "Come on in, Bill, but promise not to look at me. I'm in my workout tights." I had arrived in the middle of a workout session. Jayne and her husband, Mickey Hargitay, worked hard every day just to keep two of the most beautiful bodies in the world looking beautiful.

The stars I mentioned had a couple of things in common. They were in the public eye all the time. They had great discipline and self-image to match. That is why they were world-famous stars and stayed on top. For the rest of us, who want to live the way we do and just look like stars let me suggest a few alternatives.

Time is the great equalizer. I have settled on a program that works for me. I've watched friends and stars use it successfully over a period of time. Number one, I forget the word "diet" and start to think in terms of "way of life." I start to consciously cut down on the amount of bulk and carbohydrates. I drink a lot of water. I start every morning with fifty pushups and fifty situps. I've gotten to the point where jogging gives me a clean, energetic feeling. I work hard all day, seldom off my feet. Three times a week I go to the gym, run two miles, and do fifty situps and fifty pushups. Then I'm off to my all-time favorite relaxer, the steam room. There I perspire and love it. Out come all the toxic impurities that slow me down and clog up my system. After the shower, I lay down on one of the cots and elevate my feet while I relax for fifteen to twenty minutes. I come to the gym tired and dulled after a day of work and tension. I leave feeling like I can take on a great night of dancing and fun. I still wear the same size suit I wore twenty-five years ago.

The point is, you must do your own thing. This program works for me. You must find what works for you—tennis, golf, or a brisk walk around the block. Then do it. Do it regularly and gradually increase it. You will know by the way you feel when it works for you. As they say, different strokes for different folks, but do it.

Women have served all these centuries
as looking glasses possessing the meagre
and delicious power of reflecting the fi-
gure of man at twice its natural size.
—Virginia Woolf

19

WIVES AND LOVERS

The woman in your life can be your staunchest ally in changing your appearance to change your life. There must, however, be a realization on her part that to be successful in helping your package yourself, she must understand the motivation and thrust of your appearance packaging. She must understand that she should help package you for your business goals, not her own. Once this shift in viewpoint is accomplished, you will have a tiger on your side.

Any woman that stands up before the world and says, "I love this guy, I have chosen him above all the others, we are joining to take on the world together," can't be all bad. She can even overlook her husband's faults, and let's face it, we really need our wives' help.

Though men may claim great masculine independence and resistance to feminine help, they find it quite difficult, and somehow lonely, to buy clothes without her approval.

As we noted earlier, some men feel it is effeminate to express more than a general interest in clothing. They also feel they don't have the background or the technical information necessary to make wise clothing decisions alone. So, they take the wife along with them.

As little boys, our mothers were always picking out our clothes. Even as we grew older, Mom was there to guide us. It seemed that in no time our girl friends took over this role and soon they became wives. It just seemed natural that they would continue helping choose our clothes.

Unfortunately, the woman in your life came to this position by default. She has become the expert because there were no other experts available. From the time she was a little girl, she has been dressing dolls and she intuitively has gained a certain amount of knowledge of what clothes say about a person.

In addition, she understands when she goes to a party what everyone there has on, who is dressed right, and what their clothes say. Through her experience as the family shopper, she is the only one that has any information on fabric, color, etc., and is openly proud of her role of authority.

A man doesn't really trust the clothing salesman. His buddies know no more than he does, so his wife steps into the void with her limited technical knowledge and her vested interest as his mate. (She must realize that she is assuming a role which can make or break her husband's rise to the top.) I need not remind you that she is also his most vocal critic, and he doesn't have to be a mental giant to figure out how to keep peace in the family—simply follow her wishes. Because of her vested interest, her criticism and the other elements of her power, her influence is seen in every purchase he makes, even though physically she may not be there for the actual buying.

Most women's understanding of men's clothing is just the opposite of what it should be. The conflict in this dilemma is an intellectual one. Women dress for other women. They also dress their husbands using these same standards, forgetting that men should dress for the respect of other men, particularly their business contemporaries. She feels her clothes are a legitimate tool of social war. She feels the same way about clothes that she feels about her home and her hair styles. She does not know why she knows what she wants to say and what to wear to say it. These serve as her techniques to impress others. Openly she seeks to be a style setter and to stand above the common herd. She's not ashamed of her interest in clothes or in telling everyone about her interest in them. Society says this is okay. She would probably be a misfit if she did not. She is proud to talk about clothes and to play the fashion game herself. Her clothes are constantly talked about,so she gets a continuing feedback. This gives her guidance on her other choices and the direction of future purchases. She seems to understand that clothing reflects social position and understands what kind of woman wears what garments.

Our job then, is to shift the woman's point of view so that she can use her intuitive skills to help her man package himself to achieve his business goals. Women intend their clothes to evoke emotions in the people they meet. Men, on the other hand, play down the emotions and dress to emphasize and build positive attitudes. A woman wants attention. A man wants belief. A woman wants to be talked about. A man wants to be accepted. A woman seeks to be sensual. A man wants respect. A woman wants to be envied. A man wants to be trusted.

When the wife goes shopping for her husband, she will automatically seek to produce attention, sex, envy, and all the other provocative emotions, as if she were buying for herself. If you let her dress you, she will make you the most sexy, envied, provocative, attention-getting man who ever lost a job, a client, or a sale.

Show her this chapter and let her read the book. Then take her along to your Great Men's Store and show her what you've learned. She will love it. She will love you for doing it and she will quickly become the latest family expert on how to dress you well.

20

BE A MAN

It is now time for you to understand one of the basic reasons you are reading this book. In your lifetime you have probably experienced several different approaches to men's clothing, from absolute disinterest or seeming disinterest to the "Peacock Revolution" of the seventies. The very fact that you are reading this book means that you have matured to the point where you can conceive of clothing and appearance as a powerful tool to be used, not ignored or abused, in attaining for yourself the life you desire. Let's look at the evolution and development of the way men look at clothing.

A new father looks through the visitor's glass and points proudly at his new son; but he seldom sees the baby, at least not as a baby. What he really sees is an opportunity to fulfill all his lifelong dreams. His son will have all the things he never had. He is being given one more opportunity and he says to himself, "Son, you'll be a real man someday."

For the rest of that baby's life, phrases like "Be a man, act like a man, look like a real man," will come to haunt him but he won't know why. No one ever explained to me and probably not to many of us what a real man is, but every aunt, uncle, mother, father, cousin, teacher and principal seems to know. They pass along the dictum, "Be a Man."

As young men mature this evolves into a Pavlovic phenomenon—a stimulus-response pattern. Mention the word "effeminate" and it is like a belt in the mouth. It seems to savagely attack one's whole being and we never quite understand why. One of its effect is to dull and cut down our sensitivities to only those of a "Real Man." The real man hides his sensitivity to art, music, to beauty, and tries to avoid at any cost someone's suggesting that he's effeminate.

In the past, this was a basic reason why men displayed a very low interest in clothing. A man especially didn't want to talk to another man about dress. "Real Men" just did not talk about fashion. Like it or not, that has been an unstated objection to "clothes making the man." What a "real man" wants in his clothes is only comfort, to feel that his garments are suitable to the climate and properly fitted. Satisfaction with that alone will give him confidence.

In addition, in earlier days, there was nothing in the family budget for Dad's clothes. Once in a great while he would reward himself or do his wife a favor by picking up another gray or blue suit. But all his clothes were bought for social comfort. He had to feel at home in them. He wanted to fit in, not stand out. The "in" thing was to be a good company man, not a clotheshorse. A "real man" wanted to keep up with styles and changes, but he did not want anyone to think he was working at it. Conservatism was a characteristic of all men. They felt the same for the arts, recognizing that the classic lived on through change. Fads, because they were so short-lived, obviously lost their real value and always ended with a return to sane and conservative respectability. Depending upon their social level, men found only that they were expected to look right, never really understanding why they were wearing the clothes they wore or what their clothes said about them. They certainly never wanted anyone to feel they worked at being well dressed. They wanted everyone to think their attire "just happened." A gentleman had to choose his clothing so that nothing stood out. He kept an eye on style without appearing style conscious. Nonchalance was the approach toward men's clothes.

Another complicating factor in the way men approach clothing is that a man finds thinking about change threatening because he has built up an image of himself. That is why he becomes so antagonistic when someone criticizes him or suggests a change in his appearance. If you react to that sort of criticism, it's time to stop kidding yourself. You wear what you think makes you look good whether it really does or not. Men have developed a fear that they might be manipulated or taken by some fashion designer or salesman on the new styles and innovations in dress. Basically, they are afraid of what I call the "Fashion Game." Bi-swing shoulders, pleats, belted backs, trimming, colored stitching, Nehru jackets, Madras, are in one year and out the next. This is playing the "Fashion Game." However, you must understand that this concern about playing the "Fashion Game" is valid, because frankly you cannot win, economically, socially, or business-wise. Following the dictates of fashion puts you in the unfavorable position of being packaged by designers and fashion experts who have no idea of what you need to say about yourself with your clothing. You indicate to those you meet that you have no taste or control over your clothing habits. You simply rush hither and yon at the whim of the designers or umpires of the fashion game. You must decide what you want your clothes to say about you, and lay down your own clothing rules for packaging yourself.

Another concern traditionally held by men about clothing was the fear of duplication in dress. This concern, however, really isn't valid. If a man sees his suit on another man, it doesn't shake him a bit. In fact, he's reassured by it. I was coming out of church recently and a man said to me, "You are a man of good taste." I realized immediately we were wearing identical suits, so I said, "You, too, are a man of taste." Laughing he said, "I'm delighted to see you wearing it. Now, I know I was right in choosing it." We both walked away with a feeling of fitting in, of being "right."

Many college students in the forties and fifties had that great advantage of living, studying, and working on the same level as students from the upper social class families. They had the opportunity to study their clothes at close range. After graduation, the great equalizer, money, came along and they discovered that men's stores sell clothing to the rich and poor alike. All you need is money. They studied the "look" and acquired it. Although they did not realize it, this was a profound and potentially powerful change in men's approach to clothing. The world had changed. Anyone could acquire the right look or appearance simply by walking into a store and buying it. Unfortunately, the influence of this was diluted by the upheavals of the sixties.

Then came the revolution. Youth declared that they were not animals to be herded. They were not going to conform. And so they started the greatest conformity boom since the World War II uniform. Everyone conformed in their nonconformity. If you have ever been to a college football game and looked out on acres of blue denim cheering the squad, you know exactly what I mean. They have had little opportunity to learn much of anything about clothing.

Next came the seventies and what was called the Peacock Revolution. Out of the dark ages of white shirts came purples, pinks, chartreuse, coral, sky blue, ocean blue, red-blue, pink-blue . . . Find a color and you could find a shirt to match it. Suits were rainbow colored, with shoes, ties, and socks to match. Many men had spent years getting through school and military service and on their feet economically. They welcomed the change. It was a new freedom. Others just regarded it as "Crazy, Man." This was fun.

Finally, someone invented double-knit. You could wear it after sleeping in it and it looked fine. It was wild. Double-knit buyers were thrilled to think that they did not wrinkle. They forgot what they looked like from a conservative view-point and spent all their time hunting for a new double-knit color. As time passed, the euphoria of Christmas-in-June faded, and with it appeared large signs in department stores announcing double-knit suits tailored free during fantastic close-out sales. The passing of double-knit has been noted, and the wild colored shirts have quietly been relegated for use cutting grass, painting, or raking leaves. The colored shoes are still embarrassing us with the reality that we conservatives have again "come of age," and the tri-colored shoe definitely did not come with us.

Now do not think this is the end to fads, high fashion, and similar foolishness. Designs such as these will continue to appear as long as there are designers to create them, fashion writers to praise them, magazines to portray them, and eager young men to buy them. The one valuable thing the fads of the Peacock generation produced is the fresh new viewpoint men have about what they wear and what it says about them. I sense a new vitality and interest in his clothing from America's male. He isn't trying to prove his manhood, nor be the prettiest peacock in the yard. He is simply recognizing that his dress influences his life, and that flighty fads and fashion whims belong in that same part of the past as summer lifeguard jobs, dirt-bike hill climbs, and making love in the car.

Recognize that part of the responsibility of being a man is a mature understanding of the signals of the game. The funny clothes may get you some attention, but they will keep you out of top management. Dress like you are winning and you will be accepted as a winner. The men who run America's business dress for the roles they play. Successful men look successful. They put on the uniform of the winner. The loser has a uniform too and while they may expel great energies competing they win only against other losers.

SUMMARY

There are men and there are boys and a whole world between. Age has nothing to do with it. Packaging your appearance will determine whether you look capable or incapable, experienced or inexperienced, successful or unsuccessful. And yet it is our national peculiarity about our clothing that we plan to start dressing successfully as soon as we become successful. Remember, your appearance is truly the one factor you can control. If you package yourself to manage the impression you make on others, then their positive reinforcement will, in time, make you the person you want to be. You decide! It's up to you. If you want to be successful—look successful.

Social psychologists tell us that our self-concept refers to the mental picture we have of ourselves and carry with us for every personal, social, or business encounter and it is the catalyst that controls every evaluation of our ability, worth, and self-esteem at that moment of decision.

Everyone who wanted to and the ones who are reading this book knows and understands what success is in every area of life and what it looks like. We are exposed to it everyday like we read the time on the face of a clock, as clearly as we understand a monk's robe makes the monk.

Some of you who read this book probably remain skeptical at this point. Others are probably still outright hostile at the idea of consciously altering your appearance to control and manipulate the reactions of those you meet. Still others balk at and resent a world where they are judged by the superficialities of their appearance. To those, I must apologize. I've failed in reaching them.

To those of you whom I did reach, it has been my sincerest pleasure in sharing my thoughts with you. If you understand the main thesis of the statements made in this book, then I feel I have done some real good for my fellow man. Gentlemen, people do judge you by your appearance. Your appearance affects every aspect of your life. Fortunately, though, your appearance is the one thing you can change to alter your life. By studying and applying the principles in this book, you can achieve your business and social goals. In fact, as you've seen, you can actually become what you wear.

You now possess the knowledge and skill to control one of the most important tools of life, Impression Management. You can consciously plan the impression you make so that people will respond favorably to you. This power, like any other of course, can be abused. Yet, for the man who sincerely desires success, I'll run the risk of sharing this knowledge with anyone who will read this book.

This book has been written to help bring you and your chosen look together. I have given you in the preceding chapters the prescription. Now you must take the time to search and develop your own system of values for yourself as a human being that will give a deep personal meaning to your life. At this moment you may or may not be ready to make that "Decision of Principle" that will change your life and give your self-image its real value. We are all put here for a reason. Our job is to develop what we have and fulfill our responsibilities.

I want to leave you with a friend who will never fail you. A lot of people go to church on Sunday and feel they have recharged their spiritual batteries and can carry on for the next six days. We all sing, pray, and feel saintly; we are positive, talkative about our accomplishments and our hopes; humility is everywhere, and we have people all around us we can impress with it.

Friend, it is the cold early Monday morning alone in the

kitchen over a black cup of coffee, with your family sleeping safely upstairs, secure in knowing you can do anything. You are not alone, bow your head—He is there.

ABOUT THE AUTHOR

In his early career William Thourlby learned about the psychological effect of clothing by wearing everything from jeans to tails in movies, Broadway shows, print ads, and television commercials. Among other sterling credits he was the original Marlboro Man and one of the top ten models in the United States.

Later he expanded his interest in clothing by establishing two stores specializing in conservative suits and haberdashery, and drawing on this experience, he went on to write, "You Are What You Wear," the best-selling guide on the packaging of male executives and marketing representatives. The book catapulted Bill into national prominence as a guru to the upwardly mobile in business and industry, resulting in a new career as a lecturer and consultant to major companies as diverse as Coca-Cola and Smith Barney. He also served as wardrobe advisor to two U.S. Presidents.

Constantly revising and expanding his approach and material, Thourlby has just completed a new book, "Passport to Power," which deals with executive manners and style as well as appearance. His lively and valuable message is heard each year at conventions and as a keynote speaker throughout the country as well as scores of executive training seminars aimed at entry-level young men and women who are preparing to move up the corporate ladder. His ability to motivate and entertain at these seminars make him one of the most sought-after speakers and consultants in business today.

PASSPORT TO POWER
by William Thourlby

"PEOPLE SKILLS" "The prime factor in human capital" "The silent symbols and visual clues that powerful and wealthy people use to project and sustain power."

In this world there are two kinds of class — first class and no class. You must develop the first or you will have to live with the second. Many people go through life unaware of the consequences of how they present themselves.

The people with whom you come in contact are constantly making instant judgments about you based on the way you act and dress. The crucial first impressions you create immediately signal, correctly or not, such vital information as economic and educational background, your professional status, even your attitudes and achievements. In a society where continuous flux is the norm, background and status — because they are not written on your forehead — are difficult to gauge rapidly; the one quick indicator of who and what a person is, is the sort of impression he or she is able to project. Appearance and etiquette are the first and trusted references we use to immediately size up those with whom we come in contact. Polished manner, both in public life and in the professional world, is a key skill in achieving the advantage that's so often necessary to success. Practiced etiquette, a knowledge of what is and is not appropriate in business and social settings, will help foster a feeling of mutual respect among colleagues, superiors, and subordinates.

In my book, "You Are What You Wear," I discussed how your clothes affect other people. My premise is that you can attract power through packaging, but the other part of that package is the way you present yourself in business and society. Polished manners point to a good upbringing, intelligence, education and a sensitivity to social and corporate cues. The proper dress or packaging gets you through the door. Proper manners and etiquette show that you belong. Many people already know and practice the suggestions I discuss here, but often they are unaware of the importance or implications.

Often you only have one chance to be judged or to create a good impression. This happens over and over again in business as well as social situations. Because we come into contact with so many individuals in business and outside the office, whether or not we decide to continue an association may depend on our first evaluation. Psychologists call this "selective perception."

Selective perception is a universal method of picking out the people who are likely to interest us, or be important to us. For example, at a party of more than 50 people, no one has the time, or probably the inclination, to meet and talk with everyone there. We make instant conscious selections of those people with whom we think we might want to spend time. In business, such contacts are often handled the same way. If you are impolite or use bad grammar at a job interview, you probably will not get the job. Similarly, if you are meeting the executive of another corporation to discuss a business deal, should you display an untutored tongue at lunch or show yourself to be a rank amateur in a social situation, you may be less likely to get the contract or consummate the deal.

The way others perceive you has a direct bearing on the way you are treated. If your manners and business etiquette are not up to the standards of those higher up in an executive capacity, it is unlikely that you'll rise very far within the corporation. An executive who is unable to deal effectively with office etiquette and the established networks probably will not enlist the cooperation and support of his staff. Appearance, etiquette, and manners are key elements in the chance of success for today's professional.

(The above article was excerpted from Mr. Thourlby's latest book, "Passport to Power.)